Contents

Editor's Foreword	5
The Epiphany of Our Lord	7
The Baptism of Our Lord 　　The First Sunday after the Epiphany	12
The Second Sunday after the Epiphany	18
The Third Sunday after the Epiphany	24
The Fourth Sunday after the Epiphany	30
The Fifth Sunday after the Epiphany	36
The Sixth Sunday after the Epiphany	41
The Seventh Sunday after the Epiphany	47
The Eighth Sunday after the Epiphany	53
The Transfiguration of Our Lord 　　The Last Sunday after the Epiphany	59

proclamation 2

Aids for Interpreting the Lessons of the Church Year

epiphany

Joseph A. Burgess
and
Albert C. Winn

series a

editors: Elizabeth Achtemeier · Gerhard Krodel · Charles P. Price

FORTRESS PRESS   PHILADELPHIA

BS
391.2
.P752
Series
A/2

Biblical quotations from the Revised Standard Version of the Bible, copyrighted 1946, 1952, © 1971, 1973 by the Division of Christian Education of the National Council of the Churches of Christ in the U.S.A., are used by permission.

COPYRIGHT © 1980 BY FORTRESS PRESS

All rights reserved. No part of this publication may be reproduced, stored in a retrieval system, or transmitted in any form or by any means, electronic, mechanical, photocopying, recording, or otherwise, without the prior permission of the copyright owner.

Library of Congress Cataloging in Publication Data (Revised)
Main entry under title:

Proclamation 2.

    Consists of 24 Volumes in 3 series designated A, B, and C which correspond to the cycles of the three year lectionary plus 4 volumes covering the lesser festivals. Each series contains 8 basic volumes with the following titles: Advent-Christmas, Epiphany, Lent, Holy Week, Easter, Pentecost 1, Pentecost 2, and Pentecost 3.
    CONTENTS: [etc.]—Series C: [1] Fuller, R. H. Advent-Christmas. [2] Pervo, R. I. and Carl III, W. J. Epiphany.—Thulin, R. L. et al. The lesser festivals. 4 v.
    1. Bible—Homiletical use. 2. Bible—Liturgical lessons, English.
[BS534.5.P76]   251   79-7377
ISBN 0-8006-4079-9 (ser. C, v. 1)

8270C80   Printed in the United States of America   1-4092

Editor's Foreword

Epiphany, from the Greek word *epiphaneia,* means an "appearance" or "manifestation." The word was often used by the Greeks of a glorious manifestation of the gods, and especially of their advent to help. When connected with Christ, the Feast of Epiphany has, through the years, been connected with several different events in Jesus' life.

The earliest mention we have of the celebration comes at the end of the second century A.D. from Clement of Alexandria, who states that Egyptian Gnostics spent the night of January 5/6 as a vigil and the day itself as a commemoration of our Lord's baptism, the time of his "illumination" and "adoption" as Messiah in their view. However, by A.D. 300, the feast had established itself in the Eastern churches as a festival both of the birth and of the baptism. At the same time, it became associated with other "manifestations"—to the magi, and at the wedding in Cana of Galilee where Jesus began his ministry, according to the Fourth Gospel. The latter association with Cana may be a Christianizing of the Feast of Dionysius/Osiris and of Aeon on January 5/6, Jesus being the One who gave the true wine in contrast with the falsehoods of paganism.

Rome, followed by Africa, was somewhat slow to adopt the feast, since Epiphany was often a duplication of Christmas. However, the difficulty was solved by making January 6 preeminently a commemoration of the magi, a uniquely Western interpretation. By A.D. 450, it was celebrated throughout the West, perhaps first appearing in Gaul. At the beginning of the fifth century, Augustine also notes its worldwide observance, except among the heretical Donatists.

Following Western tradition, we now celebrate Epiphany as the manifestation of the Christ to the magi, who, in our view, represent the nations. It is, in short, a day which emphasizes Christ's universal lordly rule, a time when the church affirms its eschatological vision of every knee bent and every tongue urged to the praise of Christ the King. Yet the gifts of the magi on this day—their burial spices—inject the somber recollection of the fact that Jesus manifests his lordship only by undergoing the suffering and death of the cross.

The exegete for this volume is Dr. Joseph A. Burgess, director of the Division of Theological Studies of the Lutheran Council in the U.S.A. Dr. Burgess received his doctorate in theology from the University of Basel, Switzerland. He served a pastorate in Regent, North Dakota, and is the author of the section on Colossians in the Proclamation Commentaries volume *Ephesians, Colossians, 2 Thessalonians, The Pastoral Epistles*.

The homiletician, Dr. Albert C. Winn, is pastor of the Second Presbyterian Church, Richmond, Virginia. Educated at Davidson College, Union Theological Seminary in Virginia (B.D., Th.D.), and Princeton Theological Seminary (Th.M.), he has had a distinguished career as pastor, teacher at Stillman College, professor and then president at Louisville Theological Seminary. He has served as moderator of three different synods and as the moderator of the Presbyterian Church in the U.S. He is the author of numerous articles and of *Acts of the Apostles* in the Layman's Bible Commentary (1960), *Studies in the Psalms* (1963), and *Where Do I Go From Here?* (1972).

Richmond, Va.   ELIZABETH ACHTEMEIER

The Epiphany of Our Lord

Lutheran	Roman Catholic	Episcopal	Pres/UCC/Chr	Meth/COCU
Isa. 60:1–6	Isa. 60:1–6	Isa. 60:1–6, 9	Isa. 60:1–6	Isa. 60:1–6
Eph. 3:2–12	Eph. 3:2–3, 5–6	Eph. 3:1–12	Eph. 3:1–6	Eph. 3:1–12
Matt. 2:1–12	Matt. 2:1–12	Matt. 2:1–12	Matt. 2:1–12	Matt. 2:1–12

EXEGESIS

First Lesson: Isa. 60:1–6. Some exiles have returned from captivity in Babylon (after 538 B.C.), but many have not. In addition, the exiles who have returned do not establish the utopia they had hoped for. The walls of the city of Jerusalem have not yet been rebuilt (60:10; therefore this is before Neh. 3:1–32); social and religious conditions are far from ideal (for example, chaps. 58—59). In order to restore their hopes, the authors of Third Isaiah reinterpret what Second Isaiah had said shortly before their return from exile. These authors paint a glorious picture of a restored Zion (chaps. 60—62): they will be a nation of priests (61:6); they will be secure (60:10–12); they will prosper (60:5–7); the exiles who did not return will return through their sons and daughters (60:4, 9a; cf. 49:22–23; 66:20); and the nations will come to Zion (60:3; cf. 2:2–4; Mic. 4:1–2; Isa. 49:7, 23). Most of all, these things will take place because the Lord, not men, will do them (60:1–2). Since what the Lord will do does not refer to historical events or historical persons but is a cosmic event, this text is an example of the transitions taking place about this time from historical prophecy to apocalyptic. The hope for a restored Zion pointed to in Third Isaiah may have been written as a polemic against the priestly, concrete, and realistic program for the restoration of the temple found in Ezekiel 40—48 and written about the same time.

The text is a summons (60:1, 4a) accompanied by a description of the salvation which is coming. The epiphany of the Lord is described in terms of the sudden bursting forth of the sun at dawn, so typical in the East (cf. Hos. 6:3, 5; Zeph. 3:5; Isa. 60:19-20). "Light" symbolizes both salvation (cf. Ps. 36:9) and the presence of the Lord (cf. Isa. 10:17); it is set in parallel (cf. 58:8) with "glory," which symbolizes salvation (cf. Isa. 40:5), victory (cf. Ps. 57:5, 11), and the Lord's presence (cf. Isa. 6:3). Third Isaiah uses the prophetic perfect in 60:11, because the future event is looked at as having already taken place.

"Nations" and "kings" are drawn by this "light"; the gifts they bring are homage to the Lord (cf. 18:7; 19:21; 60:6-7; Ps. 72:10-11; Hag. 2:6-9). To "be radiant" is to reflect the light which comes from the Lord (cf. Ps. 34:5). The "abundance of the sea" is the wealth of the seafaring nations (60:9a); the "multitude of camels" is the wealth of the nomadic nations. Midian, Ephah, Sheba, Kedar, and Nebaioth (60:6-7) are nomadic Arabic tribes.

Second Lesson: Eph. 3:1-12. In many ways Ephesians depends on Colossians; in this text, Col. 1:23-27 has been used. Eph. 3:2 indicates either that Paul did not write Ephesians or at least that he did not address this letter to Ephesus (cf. Acts 19). The previous section had described the apostles and prophets as the foundation of the church (2:19-22); 3:1-12 points to Paul as the apostle par excellence, for he is the one to whom the mystery was made known first, then to the apostles and prophets, and finally through him to the Gentiles (3:3, 5, 7-8).

Paul has been given a stewardship, a task (cf. 1 Cor. 9:17; Col. 1:25), which is to make this mystery known; the word "stewardship" is the same word translated as "plan" elsewhere in Ephesians (1:10; 3:9). The gospel is described throughout this text as the "mystery" (3:3, 4, 9; cf. 1:9). The mystery is revealed in 3:6; for Ephesians the gospel is the union of Jew and Gentile into one church (cf. 2:13-22). In Greek three adjectives using the prefix "with-" bring out this unity between Jew and Gentile (3:6). This unity is God's "manifold wisdom" (3:10), which, like the "mystery," has now been made known. This is God's "eternal purpose" (3:11), now realized. In both 3:5 and 3:9-10 an early Christian pattern of "formerly—now" or "hidden—revealed" is being used (cf. 2:2, 12-13; 1 Cor. 2:7-10; Rom. 16:25-26; Col. 1:26; 2 Tim. 1:9-10; Titus 1:2-3).

This mystery was unknown to past generations (3:5), although there had been prophets who had indicated that the Gentiles would come to Zion (cf. Isa. 60:3). The "principalities and powers" (wicked angels) also had no idea of this mystery (3:10; cf. 6:12; 1 Cor. 2:8), but it has been made known to them through the church.

Gospel: Matt. 2:1–12. Matthew holds that the reality which began in the OT has now grown to its predestined fullness and will continue to be directed by the Lord. Thus the text is not intended to be taken as "history"; Matthew 1—2 is a theological prologue. The form of Matt. 2:1–12 is that of a "sacred history" made up of independent materials historicized and joined together to form a narrative. It would be incorrect to call the text a midrash, for there the written text is commented on, whereas here certain past "events" are merely illuminated by Scripture; a midrashic style of interpreting events, however, is found in this text (haggadic midrash).

The main point of Matt. 2:1–12 is to continue to bring out that Jesus (cf. 1:18, 25) is the Son of David (cf. 1:1, 2–16, 20). Jesus is born in Bethlehem, which is the city of David. The title of king is continually used for David (cf. 1:6) and when applied to Jesus (2:2) points to his being the Son of David. In 2:6d Matthew has added a line from 2 Sam. 5:2, a text about the kingship being offered to David, to the prophecy in Mic. 5:2 in order to identify Jesus as the one in whom the promises to David are fulfilled.

The magi are astrologers (priests and scholars) who play a role which supports this main point. Just as King Herod is juxtaposed to the "King of the Jews," so the "chief priests and scribes of the people," who reject the King in his lowliness and thus lose their right to be the Israel of God, are juxtaposed to the magi, who represent the religious leaders of the Gentiles and begin the fulfillment of the prophecy that the Gentiles will make pilgrimages to the eschatological sanctuary (cf. 8:11; 28:19). Gold, frankincense, and myrrh are the trappings of a king (cf. 1 Kings 10:2–3; Pss. 72:10–11, 15; 45:8–9; Song of Sol. 3:6). Gold and frankincense are offerings made at a shrine (Isa. 60:6); in 2:2, 8, and 11 worshiping is mentioned.

In Matthew 2 there is an underlying theme of Herod as the second pharaoh and Jesus as the second Moses. The guiding star (2:9) may recall the guiding pillar in Exod. 13:21. Antiquity thought an unusual star announced the birth of an important ruler, but anyone familiar with the OT would recall the star in Balaam's oracle (Num. 24:17), which the Jews had already interpreted messianically. Like the magi, Balaam was a seer from the East (Num. 22:5; 23:7).

HOMILETICAL INTERPRETATION

It should quicken the preacher's pulse to preach on Epiphany. You have a great theme: the breaking forth of light in darkness. And you have a great story, one that is known and loved by thousands who are otherwise abysmally ignorant of the Christian faith: the story of the three kings. To be sure, we have only guessed that there were three, because they brought three gifts; and the idea that they were kings comes from Isaiah 60 and not from Matthew 2; but for all that it is a story of unique beauty and power.

The other two lessons are clearly drawn to the Matthew story as a common center. The arising of light in Isaiah 60 corresponds to the rising of the star, and the coming of kings bringing gold and frankincense corresponds to the coming of the magi with similar gifts. The mystery whereby the Gentiles become heirs of Abraham and partakers of the promise in Ephesians 3 corresponds to the mysterious arrival of practitioners of an Eastern religion to worship the King of the Jews.

The juxtaposition of the three lessons makes inescapable an obvious fact which nonetheless often escapes us: our beloved wise men, kneeling so reverently in the chancel in innumerable Christmas pageants, clothed in borrowed drapery material and costume jewelry, were not part of the people of God. They were neither Jews nor Christians. They were outsiders, or as we called them in unkinder days, pagans, heathen. Just as the peoples covered by thick darkness in Isaiah 60 were outsiders, no part of Israel at all, just as the Gentiles in Ephesians 3 were outsiders, "alienated from the commonwealth of Israel, and strangers to the covenants of promise" (Eph. 2:12 RSV), so the wise men were outsiders.

But here they come, as they will when Epiphany rolls around, and the expositor's task is to relate this ancient biblical story to his or her own story and to the stories that members of the congregation are living here and now, to relate the powerful biblical symbols that surround and permeate this story to the working symbols in his or her own life and in the lives of the people who listen.

Somewhere in the sermon you will probably want to retell the story of the wise men, as creatively and imaginatively as you can. Luther's sermon on Matthew 2 is a good primer for the imagination. He describes how perplexed and disgusted the wise men were when they finally arrived in Jerusalem after their long journey. They expected to find torches lit, trumpets blowing, dancing in the streets, in celebration of the newborn King. But not a soul stirred. Even the birth of a puppy, says Luther, would have caused more excitement. Again, Luther imagines the house at Bethlehem was a tumbledown shack. There they saw nothing but a poor peasant couple with their baby. But in great, strong faith they cast out all the misgivings of common sense, fell down and worshiped the child, and presented to him their costly gifts (see *The Martin Luther Christmas Book,* ed. Roland Bainton, 1948, pp. 53–65, or *Luther's Works,* vol. 52, 1974, pp. 159–286 —both Fortress Press). On a more sophisticated level, there is much ore to be mined in the account of the wise men in W. H. Auden's *For the Time Being: A Christmas Oratorio.*

And all along, powerful symbols lie ready-to-hand in all three lessons. How have we been and how are we still outsiders? What darkness has lain or still lies thickly upon us? What are the experiences in which light has burst forth upon us like the sunrise? What star has led us into unknown paths? What gifts have we brought to the King? And how have we found in him "unsearchable riches" (Eph. 3:8)?

What is at stake here theologically is our attitude toward the non-biblical religions. How do we relate them to the finality of Jesus Christ? This problem has been thrust upon our generation more insistently than upon any generation since Constantine: As long as the world was neatly divided into Christendom and heathendom, those who lived in Christendom could leave it up to a few missionaries to worry about the meaning and value of non-Christian religions. No more. Churches stand empty in old Christendom and full to overflowing in "the mission fields." There is a Buddhist on the block, our sons and daughters are instructed by gurus, and a resurgent Islam captures the allegiance of the prisoners in our jails. There is a growing interest in astrology, magic, witchcraft—what has been called "the old religion" and is perhaps close to the religion of the wise men.

Our three Epiphany lessons unite to say that God does not despise the religions of outsiders, and neither may we. This is not to say that one religion is as good as another, but that the hunger for God is a common human trait and deserves respect wherever it is found.

At the same time, the non-Christian religions bring judgment upon us. Not one of the chief priests and scribes, whose learning enabled them to quote the text from Micah about Bethlehem—not one of them went to Bethlehem. Only the outsiders went. Only the outsiders worshiped. Only the outsiders brought their gifts.

Outsiders will not be drawn by our institutions, though we must have institutions. Outsiders will not be drawn by our personal experiences, though we must have experiences. Outsiders will be drawn by "the light of the knowledge of the glory of God in the face of Christ" (2 Cor. 4:6 RSV). That is God's hidden purpose through all ages. That is the meaning of the beloved story of the wise men. That is what Epiphany is all about.

The Baptism of Our Lord
The First Sunday after the Epiphany

Lutheran	Roman Catholic	Episcopal	Pres/UCC/Chr	Meth/COCU
Isa. 42:1–7	Isa. 42:1–4, 6–7	Isa. 42:1–9	Isa. 42:1–7	Isa. 42:1–9
Acts 10:34–38	Acts 10:34–38	Acts 10:34–38	Acts 10:34–43	Acts 10:34–38
Matt. 3:13–17	Matt. 3:13–17	Matt. 3:13–17	Matt. 3:13–17	Matt. 3:13–17

EXEGESIS

First Lesson: Isa. 42:1–7. The four "servant songs" in Second Isaiah (42:1–4; 49:1–6; 50:4–9; 52:13—53:12) form a unit by themselves. A servant was one who was bound to another, who was the servant's protector and patron. When the "servant" is linked with Israel and Jacob in Second Isaiah, he always plays a passive role; in the servant songs he plays an active role. The later servant songs indicated that the servant is Second Isaiah himself. The first four verses of the text form a unit; in it the servant is officially introduced by the Lord to the council sitting in heaven, just as a king introduces a new official to the court. The servant is not "called" at this point; his election is confirmed and his special task is described. In order to carry out the task, the Lord has placed his Spirit upon the servant like a cloak (cf. 11:2; 44:3; 61:3); thus the Lord's Spirit is not absorbed by the servant. Justice and law are more than legal terminology in this section. They refer to the total reordering of the world which the Lord is bringing about. Because the servant's message is salvation, he does not have to lift up his voice in the street like a prophet of judgment. For those living in exile who are like bruised reeds and fluttering wicks, 42:3 is a message of hope. (There is no figure here of pastoral counseling.) In 42:4a, "burn dimly" and "bruised" are repeated from v. 3, but in reverse order; the servant will have strength to carry out his task.

Vv. 5–7 of the text are part of a larger unit, 42:5–9, which I believe refers to Cyrus. The form of this unit is that of a controversy between the Lord and those exiles who doubt that this heathen king is the Lord's instrument in world history and especially in Israel's history. It begins with an introductory formula indicating a message, which is expanded in hymnic style in order to become an axiom all must accept, then cites (42:6–7) the account of Cyrus's call by the Lord, and concludes the controversy (42:8–9) by stating negatively that the Lord will not take second place to idols and positively that already (42:9) the Lord has begun to work through Cyrus. The servant song has been inserted into a context containing other references to Cyrus (41:2–3, 25; 42:5–9). "Righteousness" in 42:6 is "salvation" which the Lord has brought about (cf. 45:13). "A light to the nations" is parallel to "a covenant to the people" (42:6); just as Cyrus is to be salvation (light) to the nations, so he is to be responsible (salvation given in the covenant) for the people. The three parallel lines in 42:7 are figures indicating that the one who has been in prison is not used to the light and is like one who is blind.

Second Lesson: Acts 10:34–38. In form this paragraph (10:34–43) is a typical missionary speech or sermon from the Book of Acts (link to the situation, 34–35; kerygma, 36–42; proof from Scripture, 43a; apostolic witness, 39, 41–42; call to repentance, 42–43), although this speech varies slightly from the usual pattern (the proof from Scripture is minimal and the call to repentance is simply a report about repentance). Acts 10:37–42 is really a short history of Jesus, an embryonic gospel. Both 10:36 and 37 are introductions to this history. The words "you know" (10:36a) indicate that this sermon is really intended for Christians at a later time, for it assumes knowledge of the whole gospel, whereas the context implies that Cornelius and those with him are hearing a sermon about Christ for the first time.

The text supports the arguments in 10:1—11:18 that Gentiles were admitted into the church by Peter and then by the congregation at Jerusalem and, more importantly, that Gentiles were admitted into the church by God's intervention, for Jesus Christ is "Lord of all" (10:36b) and "in every nation" are those acceptable to God (10:35). Those who "fear God" were not a particular group but simply those who believed in the one true God and perhaps attended the synagogue. "To do right" probably meant to keep the minimum law expected of righteous Gentiles (cf. 15:20, 29; Lev. 17—18).

"Preaching good news of peace" (10:36) is a partial citation of Isa. 52:7. As in the account of Jesus' baptism in Luke 3:21-22, here too (10:38a) the Baptist does not actually baptize him, for God himself "anoints" Jesus (cf. 4:27; 10:37b, 42b). "Anointed" is an echo of Isa. 61:1-2, the quotation Jesus used in his inaugural sermon (Luke 4:18-19).

Gospel: Matt. 3:13–17. Matthew has brought out from the beginning the theological fact that Jesus is the Son of God and that the Spirit of God has been active in his life (1:18, 20, 23; 2:15). In our text this theological fact that Jesus is the Son of God is confirmed by an event which is described in terms which echo the calling of a prophet by the Lord in the OT (cf. Isa. 42:1 = Matt. 3:16b-17; Ezek. 1:1 = Matt. 3:16b; cf. Syr. Apoc. Bar. 22:1; Ezek. 2:2 = Matt. 3:16b) and the adoption as God's son of the king at his enthronement in the OT (Ps. 2:7 = Matt. 3:17; 2 Sam. 7:14). The dove was the symbol for Israel in the OT (cf. Hos. 11:11; Ps. 74:19) and in Jewish tradition; Jesus is the beginning of the new Israel by the power of the Spirit.

Matthew adds (to Mark) two verses about John the Baptist (Luke leaves him out entirely at this point). John the Baptist was a problem because he had baptized Jesus. What was the relationship between them? The question (3:14) raised by the Baptist was not an expression of politeness. At stake is not the question of Jesus' sin because

The Baptism of Our Lord

he accepted a baptism of repentance, for the question of Jesus' sinlessness is not a concern in Matthew. Jesus comes (3:13a, 14b; here this verb describes how a disciple submits to a rabbi's authority) to the Baptist, but it is clear from John's question that Jesus is not the Baptist's disciple. Matthew understood the Baptist to be Elijah, the one whose coming would mark the beginning of the end (11:13-14; 17:10-13; cf. Mal. 4:5). According to Jewish tradition, after Elijah comes the Messiah, and thus, Matthew reasons, this prophecy has been fulfilled in Jesus.

Jesus' answer is his first utterance in the Gospel; "to fulfill all righteousness" is a thematic summary of Matthew's understanding of Jesus' whole ministry. "It is fitting" points to something that God has made necessary (cf. Heb. 7:26; Eph. 5:3). "For us" includes the Baptist, for he prepares the way and thus is part of God's plan. "To fulfill" is the motto of Matthew's Gospel; Jesus is the one who puts God's plan into effect. "Righteousness" means "doing God's will" (cf. 5:20; James 1:20); Jesus is baptized by John not as one who subjects himself to the requirement of baptism but as one who through this baptism identifies himself with all who are repentant and as one who here begins to put "all" of God's plan into effect, in his whole life and even unto death. As Jesus fulfilled God's will, Matthew implies, so should those who follow Jesus (3:15 "us").

HOMILETICAL INTERPRETATION

As in the West the central lesson for Epiphany was the coming of the wise men, so in the East the central lesson was the baptism of Jesus. It is at the baptism that the light hidden in the man Jesus breaks forth to illumine us. The First and Second Lessons serve to interpret the baptism and to demonstrate its importance.

Matthew presents the baptism of Jesus as the occasion for his special endowment with the Spirit of God. In Isaiah 42:1 (RSV) the Lord says of that mysterious figure his servant, "I have put my Spirit upon him" (clothed him with my Spirit—see exegesis). And in Acts 10 the embryonic gospel (see exegesis) relates "how God anointed Jesus of Nazareth with the Holy Spirit and with power" (v. 38 RSV).

This collocation of passages clearly reflects an ancient Christology, that Jesus was preeminently a Man of the Spirit, a Pneumatic, *the* Charismatic. In his excellent little book *The Doctrine of the Holy Spirit,* Hendrikus Berkhof makes the point that before Jesus could become the Bestower of the Spirit, he had to be the Bearer of the Spirit. When the early church experienced Pentecost and its attendant and subsequent charismatic phenomena, they recognized that the fresh source of power at work in their midst was the same source that empowered Jesus in his ministry.

The portrait of the true charismatic which emerges from the three lessons taken together is an arresting one: the true charismatic makes no display, is gentle and patient, not coercive, not disdainful of the weak faith of others, willing to identify with them in their weakness, concerned for justice, persistent, doing good and battling oppression. In a time when many Christians aspire to be charismatics, there is a sermon there somewhere.

The baptism of Jesus is presented not only as his special endowment with the Spirit of God but as his commissioning for ministry. The voice from heaven says, "This is my beloved Son, with whom I am well pleased" (Matt. 3:17b RSV). And then, following the temptation, the ministry begins.

In the word of the heavenly voice, two important OT passages are brought together. The first is Ps. 2:7, "You are my son, today I have begotten you" (RSV). Psalm 2 is a royal psalm, perhaps composed originally for the coronation of a Jewish king. It was only natural that these words were understood later on as addressed to the messiah, the coming king. The second OT reference is to our First Lesson, Isa. 42:1a: "Behold my servant, whom I uphold, my chosen, in whom my soul delights" (RSV). Our English versions obscure the fact that "with whom I am well pleased" (RSV) in Matt. 3:17 is a precise quotation of "in whom my soul delights" in Isa. 42:1. In the word of the heavenly voice, two OT figures which had appeared to be unrelated are powerfully fused: the messiah and the servant of the Lord. Some scholars feel that this fusion first took place in the mind of Jesus himself. See John Wick Bowman, *The Intention of Jesus*. At his baptism, then, Jesus recognizes that his ministry must be carried out in the tension between the messianic expectations of his day and his own understanding of the servant role. Certainly the

The Baptism of Our Lord

temptation narrative that follows represents just such a tension and struggle.

Does our call to follow the example of Christ reach to even these profound theological matters? Is our baptism also a commissioning to ministry? Are we to be servants without being servile? Are we to claim the royalty Christ gives us while at the same time breaking no bruised reed and quenching no dimly burning wick? The expositor might explore such questions with profit.

The most difficult problem relating to the baptism of Jesus remains to be faced. Baptism is endowment with the Holy Spirit and commissioning to ministry, but in its primitive and basic meaning it is cleansing. Judaism in the time of Jesus was a missionary religion. It sought proselytes among the Gentiles. When Gentiles became converts, they had to be baptized. Under the old law those who had loathsome skin diseases or other impurities had to undergo ceremonial washings and sprinklings before they could return to the tabernacle for worship; so Gentile converts had to wash away their loathsome heathenism before they could worship with Jews. John the Baptist was insisting that Israel had become so rotten, so stricken with loathsome spiritual disease, that Israelites were on a par with the heathen. If they wanted a share in the kingdom of heaven, the insiders needed baptism as much as the outsiders.

Why, under such circumstances, did Jesus offer himself for baptism? Did he need to repent? Did he need to confess his sins? Did he need to wash away a corruption so deep it was tantamount to heathenism? It is a basic Christian conviction that Jesus was without sin. Small wonder, then, that the question why Jesus was baptized is raised whenever a thoughtful group of lay people confront this passage. The exegesis may be correct that this was not Matthew's problem, but it is certainly ours.

In his baptism Jesus chooses sides. He chooses to be identified with the sinful crowd, with the insiders who are really outsiders, rather than with the self-righteous Pharisees and Sadducees. He does not surrender his identity as the Sinless One, but he makes an identification with sinners. He accepts their corruption, their sinfulness as his own. He is, in Bonhoeffer's memorable phrase, "the Man for others."

The identification with sinners which he made at his baptism led Jesus inevitably to his cross. A teacher who accepts sinners and eats with them must be done away! So the words of that other servant song become true of him: "He was wounded for our transgressions, he was bruised for our iniquities; upon him was the chastisement that made us whole, and with his stripes we are healed" (Isa. 53:5 RSV).

Is being men and women for others the ministry for which we are endowed with the Holy Spirit? Is that what it means to be a royal servant? Then preach it!

The Second Sunday after the Epiphany

Lutheran	Roman Catholic	Episcopal	Pres/UCC/Chr	Meth/COCU
Isa. 49:1–6	Isa. 49:3, 5–6	Isa. 49:1–7	Isa. 49:3–6	Isa. 49:1–7
1 Cor. 1:1–9	1 Cor. 1:1–3	1 Cor. 1:1–9	1 Cor. 1:1–9	1 Cor. 1:1–9
John 1:29–41	John 1:29–34	John 1:29–41	John 1:29–34	John 1:29–41

EXEGESIS

First Lesson: Isa. 49:1–7. This is the second of the servant songs (see the First Sunday after the Epiphany above); it also begins the second half of Second Isaiah (49—55). I believe that the exiles have just returned from Babylon, and they have rejected Second Isaiah because the restoration has been so small; as a result he has become discouraged. He is like another Jeremiah, for he also is called from his mother's womb (Jer. 1:5), is sent to the Gentiles (Jer. 1:10; 25:15), and often discouraged (Jer. 17:14–15; 20:14–18). The servant is not Israel, for in 49:5–6 Israel and the servant are clearly distinguished from one another; therefore the word "Israel" in 49:3 is a later insertion into this text.

The form is that of a public announcement by a prophet of his call. There is the summons to hear (49:1a), the formula indicating a message (49:3a), and finally the word of the Lord to the prophet

(49:3). Second Isaiah adds to this form by telling of his despondency (49:4), bringing once again the formula indicating a message (49:5a) but expanded by a series of appositions to the "Lord," and finally telling what the Lord has said about a new call: the Gentiles are to be included (49:6). In 49:7 the form shifts to that of a prophetic oracle; this verse belongs to the following section.

The servant accomplishes his mission by means of the prophetic word (49:2; cf. 44:26; 48:6; 50:4; 51:16), which is effective because the Lord makes it effective (cf. 55:11; Eph. 6:17; Heb. 4:12; Rev. 1:16; 19:15). In addition, the servant is hidden (49:2; cf. 51:16), which means that he is guaranteed protection and help. Through the servant the Lord will be glorified, that is, will bring salvation (49:3; cf. 44:23). The servant, although discouraged, is confident that the Lord vindicates and rewards what the servant has done (49:4; cf. 40:27–31).

A revised task is given to the servant because Jacob and Israel have not responded to his message. What was stated indirectly in the first servant song (42:1, 4) is now stated directly; the servant is to bring the light of salvation to the Gentiles (42:6; cf. 45:20–25), who had already been summoned to listen in 49:1 ("coastlands" are the outer limits of the earth). The pun on "light" found in the RSV at this point does not exist in the original, although the OT dearly loves a pun. Since in the OT suffering is an indication of disgrace, it was a startling thing for the writer to make a positive evaluation of the servant's suffering in 49:7.

Second Lesson: 1 Cor. 1:1–9. Paul uses the standard opening (1:1–3) and thanksgiving (1:4–9) found in letters of his time, but this does not mean that the form is a mere formality, for he adapts it in order to focus on the particular situation of the addressee. Over against the Corinthians' tendency to quarrel among themselves and stress their own spiritual gifts, Paul stresses the unity of the church and what God has done. His solidarity with the church at Corinth is brought out by the fact that first he defines his status as apostle with "called," "of Jesus Christ," and "by the will of God," and then he defines the status of the church at Corinth with the same terms in reverse order: "of God," "in Jesus Christ," and "called" (1:1–2).

The unity of the church is brought out by the way Paul links the Corinthians as saints "with all those who in every place" are Christians (1:2) and by the "fellowship" which they all have with Christ (1:9b). What God has done is brought out by the extensive use of the passive throughout this text and by the emphasis on God's sustaining faithfulness in 1:8–9.

"Grace" (1:3–4) is not something abstract, for it has become real and concrete among the Corinthians through spiritual gifts, particularly "all speech and all knowledge" (1:5). In fact, their spiritual gifts have confirmed the "testimony to Christ" (1:6) in Corinth. The basic gift, however, is Jesus Christ (1:4a), who has been given to the Corinthians (1:4b). Paul counterbalances the Corinthian overemphasis on realized eschatology with the fact that they "wait for the revealing" of Christ (1:7b). "The day" (1:8b; cf. 4:4–5) is the Day of Judgment. That "God is faithful" (1:9a; cf. 10:13; 1 Thess. 5:24) is the ultimate basis for all hope.

Gospel: John 1:29–41. The text expands on prose material in the prologue; 1:29–34 describes how the Baptist is not the light but bears witness to the light (1:8), and 1:35–41 describes how through the Baptist others come to Jesus (1:7); 1:30 almost exactly repeats 1:15b. Each day (1:29, 35, 43; 2:1) the disciples grow in their understanding of Jesus until 2:11, where Jesus manifests his glory and they believe in him. Doublets indicate that the material has been combined and reworked (1:29 = 1:36; 1:31a = 1:33a; the descent of the Holy Spirit is described twice, 1:32 and 33).

John the Baptist's inferiority is clearly brought out (1:8, 15, 20–23; 3:28–30) in order to combat those who claimed he was equal or superior to Jesus (cf. Acts 18:25; 19:3). Nothing is said about the Baptist actually baptizing Jesus. The Baptist has received a divine revelation in order to recognize Jesus (1:33), and his function in this text is solely that of witnessing to Jesus. The Baptist is not the representative of Elijah, but of the OT (1:31; cf. 1:23); in John "Israel" (1:31b; 1:49; 3:10; 12:13) has a positive sense, "Jews" (1:19) a negative sense.

"Lamb of God" (1:29, 36) was linked with the Passover by the early church (cf. 1 Cor. 5:7; 1 Pet. 1:18–19; John 19:36), and the Last Supper was interpreted as a Passover. In addition, the early

The Second Sunday after the Epiphany

Church interpreted Christ's death as taking away the sins of the world (cf. Isa. 53:4-12; 1 John 3:5). Here the two ideas are combined. Jesus' preexistence (1:30), although not linked with a title, is also emphasized. "Son of God" (1:34) probably should read "elect of God"; if so, it would be an allusion to Isa. 42:1 and to the giving of the Spirit to the servant of the Lord. "Rabbi" (1:38) is the title used by a disciple to his master; it does not have the theological profundity of the other titles in this section (cf. 1:49). In the other Gospels "Messiah" (1:41) comes later and through Peter, not Andrew.

In 1:38 Jesus speaks for the first time; John intends Jesus' question to apply to everyone who hears this Gospel. "To follow" (1:37, 38, 40) means both "to go after someone" and "to become someone's disciple." "To remain" (1:38-39) has a geographical sense but also means "to be in communion with" (cf. 1:33; 15:4-7). "Come" and "see" (1:39) describe aspects of faith in John (cf. 3:21; 14:9).

HOMILETICAL INTERPRETATION

At this point the expositor who is preaching from the lectionary faces some decisions. The classic lessons for Epiphany, West and East, have been used. Although in a broad, general way the subsequent lessons deal with the revelation of the glory of God in the face of Jesus, they do not center nearly so obviously around single themes. The First Lessons form a series on the prophets and the "prophetic" passages in the Law. The Second Lessons form a series on 1 Corinthians 1—4. And the Gospels, after a final consideration of the baptism of Jesus, move on to a series on parts of the Sermon on the Mount.

The expositor may decide to preach a series of sermons dealing with the prophets. When is the last time you preached for several Sundays running on the OT? What better season for that than Epiphany? Or you may choose to do a series on 1 Corinthians. What better way to unfold the meaning of the revelation that comes to us in Jesus? Or you may choose to preach through Matthew. The Gospels are in one sense Epiphany documents from beginning to end.

Again, the expositor may opt for variety, preaching one Sunday from the prophets, another from Corinthians, another from Matthew, depending on the lesson that speaks most forcefully at the time.

Or the expositor may struggle to uncover some unifying theme, if not in all three lessons, at least in two of them.

The format of the exposition from here on out is designed to be of help for any of the above options.

First Lesson: Isa. 49:1–7. The exegesis indicates many interesting features of this servant song that will be suggestive to the preacher. One of the more striking features is the discouragement of the servant (v. 4). Is it possible to be chosen by God from birth, equipped by God, commissioned by God, and then fall into discouragement? It is altogether possible. The story of Elijah is a case in point. Or Moses. Or Jeremiah. Even Jesus knew this experience. See Mark 8:17–21; 9:19; Luke 18:8. God's answer to his servant's discouragement is not to lighten his load, reduce his commission. Instead he adds to it, makes it greater and more universal (v. 6). And he promises to the servant an effectiveness that will impress kings and princes (v. 7).

Edmund A. Steimle suggests that preaching is the interweaving of three stories: the biblical story, the congregation's story, and the preacher's own story. This lesson lends itself to such an approach. Can you tell stories of discouragement in trying to serve God that your people will recognize as their own stories? Dare you share your own discouragement? Can you then tell the biblical story of how God deals with discouragement in a way that will heal and transfigure the discouragements of people in our own time?

Second Lesson: 1 Cor. 1:1–9. Here begins a letter to a church beset by almost every conceivable sin and weakness. The church at Corinth was split into factions (1:12), full of conceit (4:8). The members tolerated gross immorality (5:1), sued each other in the courts (6:1), patronized prostitutes (6:15), toyed with idolatry (10:14), got drunk at the Lord's Supper (11:21). Times of worship were times of confusion (14:33). And some even denied the resurrection (15:12). Yet Paul calls them actual and potential saints (1:2) and offers a prayer of thanksgiving for them (1:4–9). He assures them that they are not lacking in any spiritual gift (1:7). Many of us who stand to preach could catalog an impressive list of the sins of our congregations. What would happen if instead of venting our hostility we assured them that, nevertheless, they are called to be saints and that all the necessary spiritual gifts are graciously present somewhere in the congregation?

Another direction in which one could move from this lesson concerns the future of Christ's epiphany. Although Christ's glory was revealed at the manger and at the baptism, the church still awaits a final revelation of that glory (vv. 7 and 8). Prophecies such as Isa. 49:7 were fulfilled with the coming of the magi. Yet by and large the rulers of this world are oblivious to the glory of Christ, and we await a grander and more complete fulfillment. The church is a forecast of what the world is destined to be. What we know and acknowledge will then be universally known and acknowledged. That is our hope. The Lamb of God who bears our sins (Isa. 53:7-8) will one day take away the sins of the world (John 1:29).

Gospel: John 1:29–41. John the Baptist's saying about the Lamb of God introduces one of the most powerful symbols in Scripture. It figures in the ancient Hebrew sacrificial system, in the Passover narrative and celebration, in the servant songs of Isaiah (53:7), in the Epistles (1 Pet. 1:19), and in the Revelation (5:6, 12, and throughout). It has deeply influenced Christian art and is central in the liturgy of the church. Paul Tillich says that some symbols die. In our urbanized, mechanized world, where perhaps most people have seen lambs only in pictures, can this symbol continue to live with power? Here is a real challenge to the expositor.

Another possible direction is to explore the relation between seeing and witnessing in this lesson. John sees the Spirit descend as a dove and witnesses that this is the Son of God. The two disciples go and see where Jesus is staying, and Andrew witnesses that this is the Messiah. The folly of witnessing before there has been an epiphany, before we have seen; the sterility of seeing, of receiving an epiphany, and then not witnessing!

Common Themes: All three lessons speak in one way or another of revelation, of that which is hidden (Isa. 49:2; John 1:31) being revealed (Isa. 49:7; 1 Cor. 1:7; John 1:29, 31, 34). There is a connection between Jesus' receiving the Spirit (John 1:32–33) and the spiritual gifts of his followers (1 Cor. 1:7). If you did not preach on Jesus as Bearer and Bestower of the Spirit on the First Sunday after the Epiphany, here is another chance. The emphasis on the Gentiles (nations) in Isa. 49:1, 6 relates to Jesus' taking away the sin of the world in John 1:29.

The Third Sunday after the Epiphany

Lutheran	Roman Catholic	Episcopal	Pres/UCC/Chr	Meth/COCU
Isa. 9:1b–4 or Amos 3:1–8	Isa. 8:23—9:3	Amos 3:1–8	Isa. 9:1–4	Isa. 9:1–4 or Amos 3:1–8
1 Cor. 1:10–17	1 Cor. 1:10–13, 17	1 Cor. 1:10–17	1 Cor. 1:10–17	1 Cor. 1:10–17
Matt. 4:12–23	Matt. 4:12–23 or Matt. 4:12–17	Matt. 4:12–23	Matt. 4:12–23	Matt. 4:12–23

EXEGESIS

First Lesson: Amos 3:1–8. Amos 3:1–2 begins the second section of the book, is the introduction to a collection of oracles, and states the basic theme of Amos's theology. Its form in 3:1a is that of a "call to attention" (cf. 4:1; 5:1; 7:16; 8:4), plus the identification of the speaker and those addressed. The second half of the verse is an addition, because the addressee is repeated and because the Lord speaks prematurely in the first person; the editor wanted to make sure that "Israel," which for Amos meant the northern kingdom, would be understood by later Judean hearers to include them. Amos 3:2 is an oracle of judgment; the first half gives the basis for judgment, and the second half proclaims the certainty of punishment (cf. Hos. 4:1–3).

The verb "know" means "elect"; "only" and "of all the families of the earth" indicate a selecting (cf. Gen. 18:19; Jer. 1:5). It is too much to take "know" here to mean "elected through the covenant," for Amos never mentioned the covenant. Popular piety held that because Israel had been elected, it could never be destroyed (cf. Mic.

The Third Sunday after the Epiphany

2:6; 3:11; Jer. 5:12) like the nations mentioned in 1:3—2:3. Amos reminded Israel that election required a response on their part and judgment was inevitable.

Amos 3:3–8 is an answer to those who challenge Amos's authority to speak such words (cf. 7:10–15); it is like accounts elsewhere of a prophet's call (cf. Isa. 6; Jer. 1; Ezek. 1–3). In form it is a didactic disputation. A later editor has added 3:7, a prose verse, to make sure that 3:8b is understood to mean that the Lord has revealed his plan (secret) to his prophets and this is what must be proclaimed, not that everything the Lord says becomes prophecy.

The argument is built upon an appeal to common sense, to colorful proverbial wisdom. Nothing happens by itself; every effect must have had a cause (3:3–5, 6b). In 3:6a and 8a the cause comes before the effect because fear might have many causes, but the nexus of effect and cause remains. A lion does not roar until its prey has been caught (3:4). A trumpet (3:6a) was like a siren in antiquity. It was agreed by everyone that the Lord had caused everything, including misfortune (cf. Exod. 4:11; 1 Sam. 16:14; Job 2:10; Prov. 16:4; Isa. 45:7). If so, Amos concluded, then is not the Lord also the cause of future misfortune and its proclamation by the prophets (cf. Jer. 20:7–9)?

Second Lesson: 1 Cor. 1:10–17. The reason for writing the first section of the letter (1:10—4:21) is introduced: disunity. Paul does not use his apostolic authority but appeals to a higher authority, "our Lord" (1:10a). "Dissensions" (1:10b), like "quarreling" (1:11b), is not so strong a word as "divisions" or "heresies"; Paul expects the Corinthian Christians all to hear this letter read, they still worship together after a fashion (11:17–34), and they all accept the same basic statement of belief (15:3–5), although they may differ on its interpretation.

Was there a "Christ party" (1:12)? Ultimately all would "belong to Christ" anyway, unless to "belong to Christ" was the slogan for one particular group, which seems unlikely because Paul assumes that all Corinthian Christians take Christ as their foundation (cf. 1:31; 3:10–11, 22–23). Since some "boast of men" (3:21), Paul, with ironic exaggeration, demonstrates the absurdity of boasting of men by adding the slogan, "I belong to Christ"; it is manifestly impossible to put human beings on a par with the Lord. The following verses continue the tone of ironic exaggeration with three absurd and impossible questions (1:13) and statements about baptism which indicate how unimportant it is who does the baptizing (1:14-16). In no way is Paul implying that baptism is not important (cf. Rom. 6:3-11); what is important is not by whom one was baptized, but whether the gospel is preached. "Eloquent wisdom" (1:17) can be a spiritual gift for which one gives thanks (cf. 1:5; 12:8), but here it indicates that wisdom of the world which relies on itself and thus empties the cross of its power (1:17b; cf. 2:1, 4).

Gospel: Matt. 4:12-23. The text begins with a haggadic midrash (reflection about history by means of OT passages) on the geography of Jesus' mission (4:12-17); the Matthean account of Jesus calling his first disciples follows. The text closes with a summary (4:23) which is almost identical with the summary in 9:35; these two verses become a literary framework around Matthew's summary of Jesus' words (Matt. 5—7) and deeds (Matt. 8—9); 4:23 points forward to chaps. 5—9, while 9:35 summarizes these chapters and introduces the following section (9:35—13:52). "Their synagogues" (4:23a) indicates that those to whom the evangelist is writing have separated from the contemporary Jewish community.

Matthew knew that Nazareth was Jesus' home in Galilee, but he also knew that Jesus actually lived in Capernaum (cf. Mark 1:24; 2:1). Since Jesus withdrew into Galilee after the Baptist's arrest (4:12; cf. Mark 1:14), Matthew makes use of this geographical move in order once again to point out that God's plan is being fulfilled, for "from that time" (4:17), after withdrawing into Galilee and then living in the border town called Capernaum, Jesus began to preach; Jesus was already beginning the gentile mission, for he was reaching out to Zebulun and Naphtali, "Galilee of the Gentiles" (4:15b; cf. 4:23a) and "throughout all Syria" (4:24a). In Isa. 9: 1-2, a typical Matthean formula quotation, "light" refers to the coming of salvation (cf. 5:14) and the ideal king.

Jesus proclaims the same message as the Baptist (4:17; cf. 3:2); then in 4:23 Jesus' message is described as "the gospel of the kingdom." Thus, in contrast to Mark, where the gospel is defined as

The Third Sunday after the Epiphany

"the gospel of Jesus Christ" (Mark 1:1), in Matthew the gospel is described more specifically as Jesus' teaching (4:23a; cf. chaps. 5—7) and his deeds (4:23b; cf. chaps. 8—9). In this way the evangelist brings together his major themes: gospel, kingdom, and righteousness (cf. 5:20; 6:33).

Jesus calls two pairs of brothers to be disciples. The two accounts are almost identical and very sparse. Nothing comes in the way of bringing out the exemplary obedience of those called; they follow "immediately" (4:20, 22). Healing fulfills OT prophecies (cf. Deut. 7:15; Isa. 29:18–19; 35:5–6) and indicates that Jesus is more than a teacher or prophet.

HOMILETICAL INTERPRETATION

First Lesson: Amos 3:1–8. Here we move from traditionally messianic prophecies into the mainstream of the prophetic demand for justice. The first two verses are a succinct summary of the teaching of all the prophets. First there is the declaration of Israel's election, stated in typical oriental hyperbole. God does in fact know all the families of the earth, and the prophets consistently mention other nations and God's dealings with them (Amos 9:7; Isa. 10:5; Jer. 46—51). But God's intimate, loving, caring knowledge of Israel is special. Israel is chosen and elect. With this basic premise the hearers of the prophets were in full agreement. The conclusion to be drawn seemed obvious to them: therefore God will protect us from our enemies, maintain our affluence, accept our worship, grant our wishes, fulfill our dreams. But the prophets drew a different conclusion: "Therefore I will punish you for all your iniquities!" Privilege brings responsibility. Election exposes us to the special scrutiny and judgment of God.

If we have been chosen as preachers of the word, standing in a very special relationship with God, what does this text say about our responsibility and our liability to punishment? If Americans are a specially favored people, proud of their position as most powerful nation in the world, what does this text say about national responsibility and liability to punishment?

The verses which follow are largely a series of rhetorical questions. George Adam Smith in *The Book of the Twelve Prophets* relates them to Amos's life as a shepherd in the desert. There he learned habits of careful observation, a way of inferring from a seen event an unseen cause. So God is the unseen cause of the events of history. If we preachers would be prophetic, we must cultivate a similar curiosity, a similar keenness of observation; we must be eager for God to reveal his secrets to us. As Karl Barth once remarked, we must have the Bible in one hand and the newspaper in the other.

Second Lesson: 1 Cor. 1:10–17. There was dissension and quarreling in the church at Corinth. The problem was, as Tillich would describe it, the bestowal of ultimate concern on what was less than ultimate—namely, the human leaders through whom various members of the church had come to know Christ. Now we obviously owe much to our fathers and mothers in the faith, whether the original apostles, or the founders of Catholic orders, or the founders of Protestant denominations, or the evangelist or pastor that most directly influenced us. It is right to respect and love them. But to divide ourselves from other Christians because they came to Christ through a different human influence is an excessive loyalty that approaches idolatry. It is no help for some to claim we came directly to Christ, without human intermediary, if by that claim we set up a further division, counting ourselves better than the others. See the exegesis for a different interpretation of "I belong to Christ."

It is possible for a pastor to invite, and even to delight in, strong personal attachments of members for himself or herself. It is easy for members to attach particular importance to the pastor who baptized them, whether as children of believers or as new converts. Paul was sensitive to that danger; that is why he was grateful that he had left the baptizing of new converts, with a few exceptions, up to other Christians. He is sensitive, in v. 17, that the personal eloquence of a preacher can be the basis of an idolatrous personal attachment just as easily as the act of baptism.

In *Life Together* Dietrich Bonhoeffer writes of the perils of what he calls "direct" relationships between Christians. These are relationships in which the attractive or the strong bind the weak directly to themselves rather than to Christ. Christ, says Bonhoeffer, should be the mediator of all our relationships. We should relate to each other through him.

Gospel: Matt. 4:12–23. In this lesson the Epiphany theme sounds once again: those who sat in darkness—the Gentiles—have seen a great light. The epiphany which began at the manger and was repeated at the baptism continues in the Galilean ministry of Jesus. Galilee, and particularly Capernaum, had a mixed population of Jews and Gentiles, and it is significant that the bulk of Jesus' ministry of teaching, preaching, and healing (v. 23) occurred there.

The basic message of Jesus' preaching in Galilee was, "Repent, for the kingdom of heaven is at hand" (v. 17 RSV). Do we preach repentance enough to ourselves or to our people? It means, as we know, not merely feeling guilty and sorry, but a radical change of mind and heart, a new direction for life, a reversal of values. Here Jesus stands in the line of the prophets.

There is also in this lesson the story of the calling of the first four disciples. It is an extraordinary story, and we must not let our familiarity with it blind us. No one has seen the wonder of it better than Bonhoeffer in *The Cost of Discipleship*. A quick refresher there will stimulate the preacher both for self-examination and proclamation. The call of Jesus is a word of great demand and of great grace. It demands everything and promises everything. Only such a word could liberate men, caught in the family and business responsibilities so familiar to us all, to respond so immediately and so totally.

Common Themes. Both Amos (5:14–15) and Jesus (Matt. 4:17) call for repentance. In Amos, Israel must repent because unbelievable doom is on the way: God is going to visit them with punishment (3:2). Grace is mentioned as a remote possibility. In Jesus, Israel must repent because unbelievable grace is on the way: the kingdom of heaven, that which countless generations have longed to see.

The calling of Amos to be a prophet through his sharp, intuitive insight into the hidden causes of events can be compared with the call of the four fishermen by the gracious, demanding, personal intervention of Jesus. Amos's call was not altogether impersonal (see 7:15).

The Fourth Sunday after the Epiphany

Lutheran	Roman Catholic	Episcopal	Pres/UCC/Chr	Meth/COCU
Mic. 6:1–8	Zeph. 2:3; 3:12–13	Mic. 6:1–8	Zeph. 2:3; 3:11–13	Zeph. 2:3; 3:11–13 or Mic. 6:1–8
1 Cor. 1:26–31	1 Cor. 1:26–31	1 Cor. 1:(18–25) 26–31	1 Cor. 1:26–31	1 Cor. 1:18–31
Matt. 5:1–12	Matt. 5:1–12a	Matt. 5:1–12	Matt. 5:1–12	Matt. 5:1–12

EXEGESIS

First Lesson: Mic. 6:1–8. The triple "call to attention" (6:1a, 1b, 2a; cf. 1:2; 3:1, 9) marks both the introduction to the second part of Micah and to the saying in 6:3–5. In Micah 1—3 judgment is announced to those who have "confidence" that they are safe (2:6; 3:11); Mic. 6:2–5 refers to a very different setting in which the Lord pleads (6:3) with his people, who have come to doubt his promises —a setting more like that of Second Isaiah. The form of 6:2–5 is that of a legal controversy; the mountains and foundations of the earth are witnesses. "Foundations" are the pillars supporting the edges of the world (cf. Isa. 40:21; Ps. 82:5; Prov. 8:29). "My people" (6:3) points to the covenant basis for the Lord's plea. A pause should be understood after 6:3; the people have no answer. The Lord then switches from defendant to prosecutor. In Hebrew there is a pun between "wearied" and "brought up" (6:3b, 4a). "Shittim and Gilgal" refer to the crossing of the Jordan (cf. Josh. 3:1; 4:19).

In order to tie 6:6–8 to 6:2–5, it would be necessary to imagine that the people again have no answer and that someone, convinced by the Lord's answers, speaks up with the traditional question of the penitent (cf. 1 Sam. 6:2; 2 Sam. 21:3), for he would be expected to bring an offering (cf. Exod. 23:15; 34:20). In 6:6–8 the editor has added a "Torah liturgy"; the penitent asks an authorized person, usually the priest, which sacrifice is acceptable for the penitent's sin (cf. Pss. 15; 24:3–6; Isa. 33:14b–16). The sacrifices asked about are in an ascending scale of value. "Burnt offerings" are expensive because nothing remains to be used elsewhere. "Calves a year old" are more valuable than eight-day-old calves, which are acceptable (Lev. 22:27). The "firstborn" was a forbidden sacrifice (Lev. 18:21; 20: 2-5; Deut. 18:10), although it was given in extreme situations (cf. Judg. 11:39; 1 Kings 16:34; 2 Kings 3:27; 16:3; 21:6). Here it is not meant as a real option but functions as hyperbole; it is the most valuable sacrifice imaginable.

The questions are not answered. Instead, in traditional prophetic fashion, sacrifice is useless apart from conduct and trust (cf. 1 Sam. 15:22-23; Amos 5:21-24; Hos. 6:4-6; Isa. 1:10-17; Jer. 7:21-23). Mic. 6:8b is like a catechetical summary of prophetic teaching. It is, however, an oversimplification to equate Amos with "justice," Hosea with "love kindness," and Isaiah with "walk humbly"; their proclamation was broader than these slogans. "To walk humbly" is "to live dependently." "Man" means "creature" (cf. 6:6a), not "abstract human being."

Second Lesson: 1 Cor. 1:26-31. Paul takes up an idea already mentioned in 1:20 (cf. 4:10). As an example of the contrast between the message of the cross and human wisdom, Paul reminds the Corinthian Christians of how their congregation was founded. The Corinthians who became Christians were mostly of the lowest social class (cf. 7:21; to be sure, some were better off, 11:21; Acts 18:8), but God called them anyway. The argument he uses is well-known in the OT; God does not act according to our ways of thinking but elects the small, the unknown, that which is not (cf. Deut. 7:6-8; 26:5-9; Matt. 5:3; 11:25; Mark 10:31; Luke 1:51-53; Rom. 4:17; James 2:5). Therefore there is no way to boast, because whatever they are is the result of God's grace (cf. 4:7), not their wisdom (or their works—to use terminology Paul uses elsewhere to say the same thing). Nor does this mean that the foolish, weak, and despised now can boast. Only the one who is humble is free for the only boasting possible, boasting in the Lord (Jer. 9:24; cf. 1 Sam. 2:10; Rom. 3:27; 2 Cor. 11:16—12:10; Gal. 6:14; Eph. 2:9).

From God (not yourselves, so that you could boast) you have "your life in Christ" (1:30a; cf. 2 Cor. 5:17-18). He made Christ "our wisdom" (1:30b); Christ replaces any kind of a personified wisdom which the Corinthians, using Jewish wisdom speculation, might think of as the mediator between God and man (cf. Prov. 8:22-31; Wisd. of Sol. 7:22—8:1; Sir. 24:1-12). The shift from second person plural to first person plural and the compact phrasing probably indicate that in 1:30b ("our righteousness and sanctification and redemption") Paul made use of a liturgical fragment.

Gospel: Matt. 5:1-12. According to 5:1 the listeners are the disciples, but in 7:28 it becomes evident that the listeners are the "crowds." "The mountain" (5:1) is a traditional place of revelation (cf. 15:29; 17:1; 28:16), but for Matthew the parallel of Moses on Mount Sinai is also present (cf. Matt. 2:1-12). For Matthew the Sermon on the Mount is the gospel in the gospel; the Beatitudes have been called a "little catechism" and the "entrance requirements" for the kingdom of heaven. The OT and Jewish background for the Sermon on the Mount is the wisdom tradition, which stresses how the wise individual, because he does God's will (which is love), is upright, righteous; only on the day of judgment will this righteousness be made known and rewarded.

In form the Beatitudes are a doctrinal poem made up of two strophes. Each strophe has four lines set in parallelism; the second strophe puts greater emphasis on human action. The final beatitude is a later expansion, for it is much longer and moves from the third person singular to the second person singular. The Lucan version of the Beatitudes is earlier (Luke 6:20-23); in general Matthew can be said to have spiritualized the Beatitudes.

Both strophes close with lines which refer to "righteousness" (5:6, 10). The Christian disciple is called upon to be active (hunger and thirst for, be persecuted for) in fulfilling the requirements (righteousness) for entrance into the kingdom, for then he will be allowed to enter the kingdom and receive its rewards. "Rejoice and be glad" (5:12; cf. Rev. 19:7) are terms used to describe the eschatological joy which is already present for those who are with Christ (cf. 28:20b). The two added verses (5:11-12) bring out the fact that for Matthew, Jesus is righteousness; the Beatitudes cannot be rightly understood apart from the person and work of Jesus, who takes the place of the law.

Although "the poor" (5:3) was the name for a specific social class in the first century, Matthew's concern is to describe those who look to God for help. The "meek" (5:5) are very similar to the humble (cf. 11:29), the "poor in spirit" (5:3). To receive "mercy" (5:7) seems to be the result of showing mercy (cf. 6:12, 14–15; 18:23–35; James 2:13).

HOMILETICAL INTERPRETATION

First Lesson: Mic. 6:1–8. This familiar lesson is one of the high watermarks of the OT. God has a controversy with his people so serious that the mountains, the hills, and the enduring foundations of the earth must witness it. The issue, as so often in the prophets, is that the people wish to substitute excessive religious rites and ceremonies for those qualities of individual and national life which are truly important to God. See the parallels from 1 Samuel, Amos, Isaiah, and Jeremiah cited in the exegesis. What God requires is not extravaganzas of worship, but *mišpāṭ* ("justice"), *ḥeseḏ* ("mercy"), and a humble walk with him.

The Hebrew words are important, for our English words do not plow deep enough. *Mišpāṭ* is not justice in the sense that everyone gets his or her fair share, or in the sense, so well expressed by Gilbert and Sullivan's *Mikado,* that the punishment exactly fits the crime. *Mišpāṭ* is delivering the oppressed from their oppression, rescuing the victims of injustice, setting right that which has gone wrong. *Ḥeseḏ* is not simply mercy or kindness. Luther is closer when he translates it "grace." Norman Snaith says it is "God's steady and extraordinary persistence in continuing to love wayward Israel in spite of Israel's insistent waywardness" (*The Distinctive Ideas of the Old Testament* [London: Epworth Press, 1945], p. 102). It is God's loving loyalty to his covenant. John A. Redhead's famous sermon outline captures the meaning of *ḥeseḏ*: God never lets us go; God never lets us down; God never lets us off. The people of God are called to exercise just that kind of loving loyalty toward God and toward each other.

Without a humble walk with God, even *mišpāṭ* and *ḥeseḏ* can become deadly. Reread Reinhold Niebuhr's analysis of the forms of pride in *The Nature and Destiny of Man.* There is pride of power and pride of knowledge, but pride of our virtues is worse. *Do-gooder* is a bad term. Why? Most of us want to see good done. But do-gooders think their good is final and absolute. They are deadly serious, lacking any sense of humor about their work, which means they have no distance from it, no perspective on it. They cannot see how partial and relative it is.

No amount of "religion" is an adequate substitute for justice, loving loyalty, and humility. What occasions in your life tempt you to make that substitution? What occasions in the life of your congregation? In the life of the nation?

Second Lesson: 1 Cor. 1:26–31. With v. 17, Paul's discussion of the divisions within the Corinthian church has moved into a discussion of the wisdom of this world versus the wisdom of God. In vv. 18–25 it is the *cross* which seems absolute folly to the world but is nonetheless the power of God and the wisdom of God. In our lesson, beginning with v. 26, it is the *church* which represents a radical reversal of the world's values.

In our normal, worldly way of thinking, we know that in order to succeed, the church needs members who are wise, powerful, and upper-middle-class. But God chose initially for his church foolish people, weak people, lowly and despised people—people whose very existence the world ignored. Whatever that church accomplished, it could not boast of; it could only give God the glory.

What does this say to the cultural captivity of the church in our day? Is it good that the "main-line" churches are so predominantly upper-middle-class? Is it good that the church owns so much property, is financially powerful? Should the church seek political power? Should the church follow the wisdom of this world's psychology or of its management techniques? On the other hand, should the church be willfully stupid and obscurantist? Should church people seek and enjoy the world's affluence? For examples of the cultural captivity of that branch of the church which a generation ago was almost withdrawn from the world, see the recent book *The Worldly Evangelicals* by Richard Quebedeaux.

In the midst of this discussion, Paul rises to a christological affirmation that deserves a sermon all to itself. You will find it in v. 30. See the exegesis for helpful comments on this verse. "Thou, O Christ, art all I want," sang Charles Wesley. "More than all in thee I find." Because of the sufficiency of Christ, the church can afford to live counter to the world's standards.

The Fourth Sunday after the Epiphany

Gospel: Matt. 5:1-12. Here begins a succession of Gospels drawn from the Sermon on the Mount. No part of the sermon is more familiar than the Beatitudes. One could preach a fruitful series of eight or nine sermons from them, but how can they be dealt with in a single sermon?

We could begin by considering how ridiculous they are. Anyone making a list of the truly happy people in the world would not include the poor in spirit (those hung up on simplicity of life-style? or maybe even the depressed?), or the mourners, or the meek (the nice guys who always finish last, the losers), or the hungry and thirsty for righteousness (whose tender consciences take all the pleasure out of being members of the world's most affluent society), or the persecuted. It may seem possible to include the merciful among the happy, until we remember what easy marks merciful people are, how they lack the toughness that is essential if one is to make it in this world. And the pure in heart?—there is no room for prudes in this liberated generation. As for the peacemakers, it sounds good until you try it seriously, and then you run into the real government of this world, the military-industrial complex, and you find yourself labeled unpatriotic, and even persecuted. Jesus must surely be engaging in comedy when he calls such people blessed, fortunate, happy.

It is serious comedy. Jesus really means to reverse the world's wisdom and the world's values. He really means to promise to such unlikely people the earth, the kingdom of heaven, comfort, satisfaction, mercy, the beatific vision of God, the status of God's children. These rewards are not earned because we try very hard to be meek and merciful and so on. No, it is all of grace, what Bonhoeffer calls "costly grace." In calling us to be his disciples, Christ frees us to be his ridiculous, blessed people. As the exegesis says, he himself takes the place of the law. Are we willing to accept the folly of discipleship, the reversal of the world's values? If not, we cut ourselves off from Christ's strange, comic, liberating grace. We choose to stay safely with our nets and our own support group. And we miss the only real blessedness there is.

Common Themes. Both the Second Lesson and the Gospel deal with God's choice of foolish, weak, low, despised people in order to confound the world's wisdom. Whichever becomes the sermon's text, the other can enrich it immeasurably. Even the First Lesson can be drawn in here. The world's wisdom has a place for religious display, but it has no room for those foolish things to which God attaches importance: justice, loving loyalty, and humility.

The Fifth Sunday after the Epiphany

Lutheran	Roman Catholic	Episcopal	Pres/UCC/Chr	Meth/COCU
Isa. 58:5–9a	Isa. 58:7–10	Hab. 3:1–6, 17–19	Isa. 58:7–10	Isa. 58:5–10
1 Cor. 2:1–5	1 Cor. 2:1–5	1 Cor. 2:1–11	1 Cor. 2:1–5	1 Cor. 2:1–11
Matt. 5:13–20	Matt. 5:13–16	Matt. 5:13–20	Matt. 5:13–16	Matt. 5:13–20

EXEGESIS

First Lesson: Isa. 58:5–10. By reading between the lines, it is possible to see that a debate is going on. The exiles who have returned from Babylon are torn by internal dissension; they have not even been able to restore the "ancient ruins" (58:12; the time would be the end of the sixth century B.C.). On the one hand, some, probably with priestly inclinations, hold that strict observance of worship practices will be noticed by the Lord and as a result he will restore Zion. They have strictly observed what is required (58:2–5), but they complain that the Lord has failed to keep his side of the bargain (58:2–3). The Lord points out that they may be meticulous in worship but they are also self-righteous and oppress their fellows (58:3). On the other hand, some are prophetic. The value of externalized religious practices is questioned. "*Keep* justice, and *do* righteousness" (RSV, emphasis added) is the way the section called Third Isaiah begins (56:1). True worship, true fasting, is showing mercy (cf. Amos 5:21–24; Isa. 1:10–17; Zech. 7:3–10); it is what the servant in Second Isaiah (49:9–10) and later another like him (61:1–3) actually do. Then the Lord will restore Zion (58:8–9a, 10b). Restoration is described in terms of the sudden bursting forth of the sun at dawn, as it does in the East, and in terms of speedy healing (cf.

Hos. 6:3–5; Zeph. 3:5). The relationship which had been broken will be restored (58:9a; cf. 65:24).

The form of the text is that of a salvation-judgment oracle. In 58:5 there is a summary of the indictment in the preceding verses; 58:5 is also a bridge to the next section of two verses; 58:6–7 is like the admonition in the classical judgment oracle, but 58:8–12 is a section on salvation. The structure of the argument is conditional (as in case law: "if . . . then," 58:6–9a, 9a–12). Although the text purports to apply to the nation, in actual fact its tenor is individualistic; the requirements and blessings are for individuals. Fasting in the OT was practiced in order to express penitence, mourning, and supplication; it was never an ascetic exercise. In 58:8b Third Isaiah reinterprets Second Isaiah 52:12; the story of the pillar of cloud and fire lies in the background (Exod. 14:19). The importance of freedom, an existential concern for those recently in exile, is brought out in four different ways in 58:6 and once again in 58:9b.

Second Lesson: 1 Cor. 2:1–5. Paul in his proclamation and in his person becomes an example of the contrast between the message of the cross and the wisdom of men, the theme already stated in 1:17. He asks the Corinthian Christians to remember how he did not proclaim the gospel to them in charismatic speech (2:1b, 4a; cf. 1:5; 12:8), which, when overly emphasized, would actually stand in the way of the message of the cross. He did not impress them with his spiritual power by performing mighty spiritual acts (2:3a; cf. 1:22; 4:10; 2 Cor. 12:9–12) but was with them in the weakness and fear and trembling of one who knows himself to be fully dependent on God (cf. Exod. 15:16; Phil. 2:12). To the contrary, his "demonstration of the Spirit and power" (2:4b) was the resulting faith of the Corinthian Christians (2:5). The existence of the church at Corinth was the demonstration Paul brought (cf. 9:1–2; 2 Cor. 3:2–3).

In 2:5 charismatic speech (2:1a, 4a) is demoted to being simply the "wisdom of men," because such "lofty words" may forget both that there is a basic distinction between God and sinful human beings and that the Parousia has not yet arrived (cf. 4:8). True power is not in "charismatic speech" or in the "wisdom of men," but the "power of God" and the "wisdom of God" (cf. 1:24), the cross. The perfect passive participle "crucified" indicates that Christ continues to be present as the one crucified (2:2b; cf. 1:17, 23; Gal. 3:1). To preach "nothing" except the cross (2:2b), which destroys every kind of false "wisdom" man holds about himself and God, was not a departure from Paul's usual proclamation; it is the center of his gospel.

Gospel: Matt. 5:13–20. Matt. 5:13–16 is a transitional section between the Beatitudes and the discussion of the place of the law; 5:16 is a summary. The first two parables sound a note of promise; salt cannot lose its taste and a city on a hill cannot be hid. But 5:13b and 15 sound a note of exhortation (cf. 25:14–30). This section points to the universal mission to be carried out by the disciples (5:14a "world"; 5:15b "all"; cf. 28:19).

Matt. 5:18 is a very strict statement about the law. But in 28:19 the command is given to make disciples of all nations, which means that circumcision and thus the Mosaic law have been abrogated. How can these two positions be reconciled? Matthew faced a situation made up of both indifference and Christian pharisaism. He was concerned that the Christian faith be lived but did not want to be trapped by the legalism of the past; in solving this problem, he made use of traditional materials from the controversies over the law which had been going on in his area, probably eastern Syria.

In 5:18a, "till heaven and earth pass away" does not mean "never," as can be seen from 24:35a, but the end of history; "until all is accomplished" (5:18b) sets another limit to what 5:18a means, as can be seen by 24:34, where the limit is "this generation." In 5:18b "until all is accomplished" refers, in typical Matthean fashion, to the fulfillment of OT prophecies in Jesus' whole career, most particularly in his death and resurrection, which is the apocalyptic end of history as well as the new beginning. Because this end has taken place, the law for the Christian is no longer the Mosaic law but "all that I have commanded you" (28:20a). Because Jesus takes the place of the Mosaic law, he may either radicalize or abrogate it (cf. 5:21–48).

Matt. 5:17 belongs to the same perspective. Both "the law and the prophets" point forward to Jesus Christ, who has fulfilled them and taken their place. Matt. 5:19, in form a double statement of "holy law," represents the position of the moderates in the Matthean situation; "least" does not mean exclusion from the kingdom, but merely less honor. Different levels in the kingdom are mentioned elsewhere

The Fifth Sunday after the Epiphany

in the NT (cf. Mark 10:35-40; Luke 12:47-48; 1 Cor. 3:12-15). As is usual in Matthew, the emphasis is on doing and teaching. Matt. 5:20 both summarizes 5:17-19 and introduces the next section. "Righteousness" is a requirement for the kingdom, yet does not mean a greater pharisaism but Christ's way.

HOMILETICAL INTERPRETATION

First Lesson: Isa. 58:5-10. Our prophet, whoever he was, moves on the same high level that we found in Micah last Sunday. There is the same impatience with a religion of mere outward forms (in this case fasting); the same tilt toward the oppressed, the hungry, the poor, the naked; the same demand for justice and loving loyalty; the same insistence that if we do not love our neighbors, we cannot claim to love God. Nowhere else does the OT come so close to the words of Jesus in Matt. 25:31-46. The relevance of this passage to such current problems as world hunger and the millions of refugees is obvious.

What is particularly notable here is the promises given to those who keep the true fast. "Your light shall break forth like the dawn." Here the Epiphany theme of light breaking forth in darkness sounds once again. Could keeping the true fast mean an end to our personal, congregational, and national darkness? "Your healing shall spring up speedily." An end to our personal, congregational, and national sickness? "Your righteousness shall go before you, and the glory [another Epiphany word] of the Lord shall be your rear guard." What a parade! An end to going around in aimless circles? "Then you shall call, and the Lord will answer; you shall cry, and he will say, Here I am." An end to the decline and dearth of prayer, personally, congregationally, nationally? An end to the absence of God (see 58:3)? There is no blanket promise here that we will receive whatever we cry for. God promises the best of all gifts: himself. "What do you desire?" the Lord asked one of his great saints. *"Nihil nisi te*—nothing except thyself" was the reply.

Second Lesson: 1 Cor. 2:1-5. Paul continues to contrast the world's power and wisdom with God's power and wisdom. This time the center of attention is his own preaching—the preaching he did when he first came to Corinth. That preaching did not commend itself by the kind of eloquence the world enjoys (lofty words) or by the kind of argument the world understands (plausible words). It was the unadorned declaration of what the world regards as utter folly, the word of the cross (see v. 18). Paul's preaching was marked by weakness, fear, and trembling. Yet it came through with an unworldly power, the power of the Holy Spirit.

Here is a lesson that needs to be applied totally to the preacher before any application to the congregation is sought.

Gospel: Matt. 5:13–20. If we can take the gracious promises in the Beatitudes as the key to the entire Sermon on the Mount, then the sermon is not, as Luther feared, a second law and Christ a stricter Lawgiver than Moses. It is a proclamation of grace, costly grace to be sure, but grace which enables us to be what we really are not and to do what we really cannot do. Augustine's prayer may be the best commentary on the Sermon on the Mount: "Give what thou demandest and demand what thou wilt."

"You are the salt of the earth." Here is a gracious word. You who are foolish, weak, despised, low, virtually nonexistent are by my grace the salt of the earth. There is a demand: that we not lose our saltiness, our ability in hidden, quiet ways to flavor the earth and to preserve it from putrefaction. And there is a promise: that by God's grace we will not lose our saltiness.

"You are the light of the world." Another gracious word. You who are poor in spirit, who mourn, who hunger and thirst, who are persecuted, and all the rest are by my grace the light of the world. The demand: that we not hide our light, that we be vulnerable as a city set on a hill. The promise: that the light of our good works will lead the world to give glory, not to us but to our Father in heaven. Light and glory are Epiphany words. The promise is that we unlikely disciples may become ourselves little epiphanies of the glory of God.

The graciousness of the sermon is not so evident in vv. 17–20, but it is there. Christ does not abolish the law and the prophets by relaxing their strenuous demands. Neither does he abolish the gracious promises of the prophets, like the ones in Isaiah 58. And he does not abolish the gracious aspects of the law which are celebrated in passages like Psalm 1, Ps. 19:7–11 and Ps. 119. Our righteousness must exceed the righteousness of the scribes and Pharisees, not by observing the letter of the law more scrupulously but by understanding and obeying its total spirit (see what follows in the rest of Matt. 5). And this understanding and obedience come not by our strenuous efforts but by God's liberating grace which makes us meek, hungry for righteousness, merciful, pure in heart, and so on.

Common Themes. In Isa. 58:8 righteousness is a gift, God's gracious reward to those who keep the true fast. So it is in Matt. 5:20. Only a graciously given righteousness could possibly exceed the righteousness of the scribes and Pharisees, who stood on the pinnacle of human moral effort. An interesting parallel is in Matt. 25:37, where the righteous are unaware of their righteousness!

In Isa. 58:8 and 10 light is likewise God's gift, his gracious reward. So also the light which the disciples are and have in Matt. 5:14–16 is given to them. It is grace.

Finally we may say that Paul in his preaching was able to be salt and light to the church at Corinth precisely because he did not rely on human effort, but on the power of God.

The Sixth Sunday after the Epiphany

Lutheran	Roman Catholic	Episcopal	Pres/UCC/Chr	Meth/COCU
Deut. 30:15–20	Sir. 15:15–20	Sir. 15:11–20	Deut. 30:15–20	Deut. 30:15–20 or Sir. 15:15–20
1 Cor. 2:6–13	1 Cor. 2:6–10	1 Cor. 3:1–9	1 Cor. 2:6–10	1 Cor. 2:6–13
Matt. 5:20–37	Matt. 5:17–37 or Matt. 5:20–22, 27–28, 33–34, 37	Matt. 5:21–24, 27–30, 33–37	Matt. 5:27–37	Matt. 5:20–37

EXEGESIS

First Lesson: Deut. 30:15–20. King Josiah did not use the present Book of Deuteronomy for his reform (621 B.C.), but probably an earlier edition (Deut. 5—28; cf. 2 Kings 22:3—23:3, 21–23). Some parts of the book, including this text, are probably from the

Exile (cf. 4:27–31; 30:3–6). Deut. 30:15–20 is part of the third section of the book, the making of the covenant in the land of Moab (29—32). The covenant in Moab should be understood as a renewal and extension of the covenant at Sinai (cf. 31:10–13; Josh. 24; 1 Sam. 12). It is even probable that the pattern used in Near Eastern covenant treaties (preamble, past history, basic principles, document clause, gods as witnesses, and curses and blessings) is reflected in the structure of Deuteronomy 29—30 (29:2–9, the past saving acts of the Lord; 29:10–15, the solemn charge to enter into the covenant; 29:16–28, curses on those who break the covenant; 30:1–10, blessings and restoration for those who return to the covenant; 30:11–20, appeal to choose the covenant with the Lord, including 30:9, heaven and earth as witnesses and again a blessing and a cursing).

"This day" occurs three times in this text and very frequently throughout Deuteronomy; it is a liturgical expression and means "every day." Israel is faced with the necessity of constant decision. It cannot simply look to the past, but is called upon to make this past present in both worship and life. "Good" is a word often used by the prophets to describe the Lord's requirements (Isa. 1:17; Amos 5: 14–15; Mic. 3:2; 6:8a); it is not a philosophical idea but the sum of the commandments and equivalent to the first commandment (Exod. 20:2–3).

The second meaning of "good" in this text is "prosperity." "Life," which stands in parallel with "good," is very material and concrete in Deuteronomy; its highest expression is the "land," which will furnish everything for Israel and make it prosperous. The opposite, death and evil, is therefore exile (cf. 30:18; 4:26; 11:17; 28:21) and ultimately destruction (cf. 6:15; 8:19–20). "Blessing and curse" (30:19) are ultimate sanctions. "Heaven and earth" (30:19) are witnesses (cf. 4:26; 32:1; Isa. 1:2; Jer. 2:12), obviously for Israel not as gods but as traditional elements in the covenant pattern. "Love" (30:16, 20) for Deuteronomy is to be spontaneous, personal, and total (cf. 6:5; 10:12; 11:13; 13:3); it is not a kind of feeling but a doing, an obeying (30:16, 20). The law is the guide which spells out how this love should be lived (cf. 4:7–8; 6:4–9).

Second Lesson: 1 Cor. 2:6–13. In this text Paul once again takes up the argument from 1:18–25. The "wisdom of God" (2:6–7) was discussed in 1:24 (cf. 1:30); the "wisdom of this age" (2:6b) is the same as the "wisdom of the world" in 1:20 (cf. 3:19). But he also once again takes up the problem of disunity with which he began the letter (1:10–17), for 2:6–13 is part of a larger section which again talks about "jealousy and strife" (3:3) and groupings within the congregation (3:4–6). "Mature" (2:6a) and "spiritual men" (3:1; cf. 2:12, 15) are probably terms used by Paul's opponents as they boast about their superiority (their "wisdom") and, as a consequence, quarrel (1:11) among themselves. Paul takes over their terms and uses them in an ethical sense (cf. Wisd. of Sol. 2:21–22; 1QS 5:23–24; Gal. 6:1; Phil. 3:15) in order to argue, once again with a touch of irony (cf. 1:13), that his opponents are really "babes" and even "men of the flesh" (3:1, 3; cf. 2:14) because of their quarreling.

The truly "mature" boast of no superiority for themselves, for they know the truly "secret and hidden wisdom" (2:6–7), the cross (2:8b; cf. 2:2), which allows for no boasting (1:29, 31). This wisdom has been made known to the mature by the Spirit (2:10a, 12a), who alone knows the very mind of God (2:10b, 11b), just as, by analogy, only a man's spirit knows what his inner thoughts are (2:11a). Even the evil spirits did not know this wisdom; the cross seemed to be a victory for the "rulers of this age" (2:6b, 8a), but it was really their defeat. The one who has the "spirit of the world" (2:12a; cf. 2:14) cannot understand (have wisdom concerning) the things given by God (the cross, 2:6a, 7), but by the Spirit the truly mature understand what things are given by God (2:12b), preach by the power of the Spirit (2:12a; cf. 2:5), and distinguish the spirits (2:12b; cf. 12:10). For the pattern "hidden—revealed" (2:7–10), see the Second Lesson for the Epiphany of Our Lord, above.

Gospel: Matt. 5:20–37. Matt. 5:20 is the theme not only of the following antitheses (5:21–48) but also for the rest of the Sermon on the Mount. In form it is a statement of "holy law." "Your righteousness" is that which the disciple must do in order to enter into the kingdom of heaven. It must "exceed" that of the scribes and Pharisees, but that does not mean quantitatively. What Jesus demands is a new, radical, eschatological kind of obedience based on himself. Jesus takes the place of the law. The disciples are "to observe all that

I have commanded you" (28:20a). What this implies begins to be spelled out in the following six antitheses.

In the NT an impersonal passive such as "it was said" (5:21a) introduces something God has done. "Men of old" means the generation at Mount Sinai, as the quotations from the OT indicate. "But I say to you" is an astonishing claim; by abrogating parts of the Torah Jesus puts himself above the revelation at Mount Sinai (cf. 1:23; 11:25–27; 28:20b).

In the first antithesis the triad (5:23) builds up to a climax; to call someone *raca* is to question whether he is human, a person; to call someone "fool" is to question his relationship with God (cf. Ps. 53:1). The radical nature of Jesus' demand comes out in 5:23; not my own but my brother's problem requires that I seek reconciliation.

The second antithesis (5:27–28) says nothing which is not already found in Jewish tradition, but Jesus presupposes strict monogamy for all and not merely for those who are especially pious. The radical nature of Jesus' demand comes out in 5:29–30 (cf. 18:8–9; Mark 9:43–47). The third antithesis (5:31–32) nearly abrogates the Mosaic law (Deut. 24:1–4); the more original form of 5:32 is found in Mark 10:11 and Luke 16:18 (cf. 1 Cor. 7:10–11), which do not contain the phrase "except on the ground of unchastity." This phrase was probably added to modify the originally more radical demand.

The fourth antithesis (5:33–37) begins with a composite statement from the Mosaic law (cf. Lev. 19:12; Num. 30:3; Deut. 23:21–23); Jesus clearly forbids all oaths, and thus 5:37 is not the one exception (cf. James 5:12). Oaths are forbidden because they produce a casuistic approach to truth and life; the words of a disciple, by contrast, can be depended on simply because he says them.

HOMILETICAL INTERPRETATION

First Lesson: Deut. 30:15–20. Moses was not only the great Hebrew lawgiver, but he was, according to one tradition, the greatest prophet (Deut. 34:10). In the magnificent address which is placed on his lips in Deuteronomy 29—30, we are still listening to the prophetic tradition. Again and again the prophets call upon Israel to make a choice on which their destiny will depend. The choice in our

The Sixth Sunday after the Epiphany

lesson is between life and death, between good and evil, between obeying and turning away, between blessing and curse.

We do not have to stand on the plains of Moab at some dramatic juncture in the world's history to face that choice. We face it every day. (So did Israel—see the exegesis.) In small, imperceptible ways we vote hourly for life or for death. We vote to get up or to stay in bed, to go out among people or to withdraw, to make a decision or to drift, to take painful risks or to seek comfortable security, to grow or to stay the same, to get involved or to play it safe, to be honest or to be popular, to do justice and practice loving loyalty and walk humbly before God or to be religious, to share bread with the hungry and bring the homeless poor into our house or to hide ourselves from our own flesh, our common humanity with others. Those votes, as Moses observed, are votes to love God, walk in his ways, and keep his commandments, or votes to turn away and worship false gods. And the sum total of our votes decides the course of our nation more surely than a presidential election.

One of the finest illustrations of what happens when people decide to vote for life instead of death is the book by Ernest Gordon called *Through the Valley of the Kwai*. It is the story of how life came back to a group of Scottish prisoners of war interned by the Japanese during World War II. An entire sermon on the choice of life can be built around that one, long, graphic illustration.

Second Lesson: 1 Cor. 2:6–13. Paul admits that there is a Christian wisdom and distinguishes it from the wisdom of the world. It is God's own wisdom, prepared for us. We could never conceive of it by ourselves. It can be taught us only by the Spirit of God.

Here let the preacher meditate on her or his own need to be taught by what Calvin called the *interior magister,* the inward Teacher. Then perhaps the congregation can be reminded, sensitively yet powerfully, of their need for the same Instructor.

Gospel: Matt. 5:20–37. The Sermon on the Mount now proceeds to describe that righteousness which exceeds the righteousness of the scribes and Pharisees, a righteousness which must be given us by God.

True righteousness goes beyond the commandment not to kill and roots out the hatred and contempt that lie deep in the heart and that make us all potential murderers (vv. 21-22). True righteousness seeks reconciliation (vv. 23-26). To pursue reconciliation is to find the positive meaning of the commandment against murder. We can do this because the call of Christ has graciously liberated us to become peacemakers (see v. 9). Jesus stands with the prophets in making the active pursuit of reconciliation more important than external acts of worship (vv. 23-24).

True righteousness goes beyond the commandment not to commit adultery and roots out the lust that lies deep in the heart and makes us all potential lechers. This is not the normal sexual urge but the willingness to use another human being merely as a means to satisfy our own desires. Matthew appends a hard saying from Mark 9:43-48 to emphasize that this rooting out of lust must be ruthless and resolute, and follows that with another Marcan saying about divorce (compare Matt. 5:31-32 with Mark 10:11-12). To what extent does lust lie at the root of the excessively high divorce rate in our society? We can do the impossible and root it out because the call of Christ has graciously liberated us to become pure in heart (v. 8).

True righteousness goes beyond the prohibition of false swearing, a habit that exposes us all as potential liars and deceivers. True righteousness seeks integrity. Persons of integrity need no oaths to give their promises surety or their opinions force. Their word is their bond and their "yes" or "no" is sufficient.

If we are at all correct in the above exposition, then preaching from the Sermon on the Mount ought never to be a heavy guilt trip, emphasizing how far short we all fall of an impossible set of requirements. It is rather the alluring picture of a world free from hatred and contempt, lust and lies, a world to which Christ continually calls us and for which his grace continually liberates us.

Common Themes. The world of the Sermon on the Mount is indeed a world "no eye has seen, nor ear heard, nor the heart of man conceived" (1 Cor. 2:9 RSV). Small wonder so many interpreters have seen the Sermon as an *Interimsethik,* practical only if the end of the world is immediately upon us, or as applicable only to the kingdom age at the end of time. The spirit of this world does not understand it; only the Spirit of God (1 Cor. 2:12). To choose that world is to choose life (Deut. 30:19).

The Seventh Sunday after the Epiphany

Lutheran	Roman Catholic	Episcopal	Pres/UCC/Chr	Meth/COCU
Lev. 19:1–2, 17–18	Lev. 19:1–2, 17–18	Lev. 19:1–2, 9–18	Lev. 19:1–2, 17–18	Lev. 19:1–2, 9–18
1 Cor. 3:10–11, 16–23	1 Cor. 3:16–23	1 Cor. 3:10–11, 16–23	1 Cor. 3:16–23	1 Cor. 3:10–11, 16–23
Matt. 5:38–48	Matt. 5:38–48	Matt. 5:38–48	Matt. 5:38–48	Matt. 5:38–48

EXEGESIS

First Lesson: Lev. 19:1–2, 17–18. Much of Leviticus 19, because of the ban on mediums and wizards (19:26, 31; cf. 1 Sam. 28; Isa. 8:19; 2 Kings 21:6; 23:24), probably originated in an anti-Canaanite milieu and thus in preexilic times. In one sense Leviticus 19 is a diverse collection of laws dealing with daily life. In another sense Leviticus 19 is a unity, for it has a general introduction (19:2) and a general conclusion (19:37), with a short general statement (19:19a) dividing the chapter in two, and a refrain ("I am the Lord your God") tying it all together, although the refrain begins already in Leviticus 18. Leviticus 19 is intended by the editor to be a counterpart to the Decalogue in Exodus 20 and Deuteronomy 5; 19:2b is clearly parallel to Exod. 20:2a.

The theme which unifies the chapter is holiness; because the Lord is holy, the Israelites are to be holy. Holiness by itself means simply being different, separate (cf. 20:26). But in the context of this chapter holiness becomes less abstract and negative; it stands in opposition to idols (19:4, 26–29, 31) and for social justice (19:9–18, 32–35). It is not an ethical category, for ritual and ethical commands are mixed together. As the true God, the Lord is different from idols, and his people are holy when they live according to his will and thus confirm their "differentness" from all other people.

In 19:17 inner feelings of hate are proscribed. The disagreement should be talked out, probably "in the gate," that is, in a legal forum (cf. 19:15a). And if this does not settle the matter, revenge and grudge bearing are proscribed, for "you shall love your neighbor as yourself." Various terms are used for "neighbor" in 19:15-18, but they mean basically the same thing, the "sons of your own people" (19:18a). Love of oneself becomes the standard by which one knows how to love one's neighbor.

The love command is extended to the sojourner in 19:33-34 (cf. Isa. 56:3; Jer. 22:3; Ezek. 22:7); sojourner, to be sure, here means one who has in the meantime joined the Israelites. This love is not to be simply a matter of feeling or good intentions, for it means to avoid anything which does wrong to the sojourner (19:34). The basis for such love is that the Lord loved the Israelites when they were strangers in Egypt (cf. Exod. 22:21; 23:9; Deut. 10:19; 24:17-18). An even broader basis for treating others as oneself is found elsewhere in the OT in the common creation of all persons by God (cf. Isa. 58:7b; Job 31:13-15).

Second Lesson: 1 Cor. 3:10-11, 16-23. Paul has been using imagery from agriculture (3:6-9) but switches to the imagery of building (3:9b); to use these two kinds of imagery together is traditional (cf. Deut. 20:5-6; Jer. 1:10; Eph. 2:20-21). In 3:10-11 Paul defends his apostolic authority against those in Corinth who would change what he had preached there (cf. 3:6; 4:15; 9:1-2; Gal. 1:6-9). Christ alone is the norm, the foundation (cf. 1:22; 2:2; 2 Cor. 4:5; Eph. 2:20-21; 1 Pet. 2:6).

The image shifts to that of the holiness of God's eschatological temple (cf. Isa. 28:16), the church filled with God's Spirit (cf. 1 Pet. 2:5; 1 Cor. 6:19; 2 Cor. 6:16-17; Rev. 21:22). Then Paul makes use of the divine law of eschatological retribution against the one who defiles this temple (3:17a). He probably is referring to concrete threats to the spiritual health of the church at Corinth.

In the last section of this text Paul draws together what he has been writing about the problem of disunity from 1:10 up to this point. Familiar items recur (for 3:18, see 2:6; for 3:19-20, see 1:20; for 3:21, see 1:29, 31; for 3:22, see 1:12; 3:4). He is not praising folly as a human effort (3:18b), but the folly of Christ crucified (cf. 1:22, 25; 2:2). Paul closes (3:21b-23) with a crescendo reminiscent of Rom. 8:31-39; because Christ is God's, and you are Christ's, therefore all things are yours. Christ is described as subordinate to God (cf. 1:30; 11:3; 15:28), but in 8:6 "God the Father" and "one Lord Jesus Christ" are parallel to one another. Obviously Paul has not worked out the systematic implications of all of these expressions, and each one has to be understood in terms of its polemical or rhetorical context.

Gospel Matt. 5:38-48. The fifth antithesis (5:38-42) clearly abrogates part of the Mosaic law (cf. Exod. 21:24; Lev. 24:20; Deut. 19:21). This ancient and well-known "law of retribution" is really the basis for all law codes. Jesus requires of his disciples an entirely different "way" of life, one that is bewildering to common sense and self-preservation. His disciples are to suffer injustice and not to resist evil. The presupposition is that the Lord is in control and "with" his disciples (cf. 28:20b; Rom. 12:17-21; 1 Cor. 13:3-7). Matt. 5:40 rejects the legal protection for the poor found in Exod. 22:26-27; it is better to depend on the mercy of the Lord. Jews could be requisitioned as carriers by Roman soldiers for up to one mile (5:41; cf. 27:32); the Zealots urged their compatriots to resist such demands. At first glance Matt. 5:42 seems anticlimactic and hardly seems different from Deut. 15:7-11, but Jesus has broadened this OT text, which speaks of "brothers," to include everyone.

The sixth antithesis (5:43-47) begins with the famous phrase from Lev. 19:18 about loving your neighbor. To "hate your enemy," however, is not found in the OT or the rabbinic tradition, although to "love all the sons of light" and to "hate all the sons of darkness" is found in Qumran (1QS 1:9-10; cf. Ps. 139:19-22). To "love your enemies" in the sense that everyone is included was a totally new demand (cf. 25:31-46). Nor is this love to be understood as a change of attitude or feeling toward the enemy, a kind of "stoic" love, for as the parallel sentence shows and as Matthew always emphasizes, it is action, doing, and in the first place, prayer. "Sons" (5:45) are to be like their Father, who does not distinguish between neighbors and enemies. Love for "those who love you" (5:46a) is no "more" (5:47a) than others do, even tax collectors and Gentiles; the "more" in 5:47a concludes the antithesis but also points back to "exceeds" in 5:20, the thematic verse which begins the antitheses.

Matt. 5:48 is a conclusion ("therefore"), a summary of the antitheses, and an imperative which includes a promise ("you shall be perfect"). To be "perfect" is not a quantitative measurement (cf. on 5:20 under the Gospel for the Sixth Sunday after the Epiphany, above) but means to be wholehearted, undivided. To be "perfect" is also not an abstract ideal but doing what "your heavenly Father" does (cf. 5:45; Luke 6:36, "merciful"; James 1:4; 3:2). To be "perfect" is what is demanded of every disciple, not just a few, and means the kind of action which is expected of every disciple.

HOMILETICAL INTERPRETATION

First Lesson: Lev. 19:1–2, 17–18. The exegesis tells us that Leviticus 19 is intended by the editor to be a counterpart to the Decalogue in Exodus 20. It is part of the "The Holiness Code," and its theme is set in the first two verses: the character of God's people should reflect the character of God. An interesting corollary follows: whatever the character of a people reflects, that is their real God. If a people is materialistic, their real god is money. If a people is militaristic, their real god is national security. If a people is holy, their real god is the Holy God.

One might suspect that the holiness of God's people would consist in their worship, and there are provisions in the chapter for worship (vv. 5–7, for example). But soon we move into leaving part of the harvest for the poor, not dealing falsely, not withholding wages, not mistreating the deaf and blind, judging righteously, and giving testimony honestly (vv. 9–16). We are in the presence of the basic prophetic idea of *mišpāṭ* ("justice").

Our lesson resumes with vv. 17–18, and we find ourselves in the presence of that other prophetic theme: *ḥeseḏ* ("loving loyalty"). Within the community of God's holy people there must not be unspoken hatred: conflict must be laid on the table and settled openly and reasonably; so there will be no nurtured grudges and no revenge. From the most ancient times, human beings have been familiar with the principle of disproportionate revenge: Lamech sings in Gen. 4:24, "If Cain is avenged sevenfold, truly Lamech seventy-sevenfold" (RSV). This principle still marks some family feuds and border warfare between some nations. It was an advance in the rule of law when the principle of proportionate revenge was introduced: eye for eye, tooth for tooth (Exod. 21:24; Lev. 24:20). The Holiness Code moves to new ground: no vengeance at all, not between members of the community of God's holy people.

To this point the justice and loving loyalty of God's people have been described mainly in negative prohibitions. Now comes the positive command that underlies them all: you shall love your neighbor as yourself.

An OT sermon may well be in order this Sunday. Perhaps it is only as we begin to practice the Holiness Code—and our common life still falls far short of that—that we can even begin to hear the liberating grace of the Sermon on the Mount, which is even more radical.

Second Lesson: 1 Cor. 3:10–11, 16–23. After his long digression on the wisdom of this world and the wisdom of God, Paul returns in chap. 3 to the problem of divisions in the church at Corinth. Factions should not be formed around various church leaders, he says, for they are only God's servants through whom you believed, and each was acting as God assigned him to act (v. 5). Paul uses an agricultural illustration: "I planted, Apollos watered, but God gave the growth" (v. 6 RSV). As our lesson begins he switches to an illustration from building construction: I laid the foundation, and Apollos and others are erecting the superstructure. The word "foundation" deflects him from the point that all the builders are worthy of equal honor. Instead, he says there can be many different superstructures—different theologies, different politics, different emphases in ministry—but the foundation is always the same: Jesus Christ. A suitable text for an ecumenical age.

The construction illustration leads in vv. 16–17 to a favorite Pauline metaphor for the church: God's temple in which the Holy Spirit dwells. And this temple is not constructed of gold, silver, precious stones, wood, hay, stubble, but of living people, the members of the church, the holy people of God. See the exegesis for many parallel passages.

Beginning in v. 18, Paul brings together the two themes that have occupied him thus far: to boast of men is a form of worldly wisdom, not the wisdom of God.

Then comes one of the great texts (21b–23). Everything belongs to you. You do not belong to Paul: Paul belongs to you. So with Apollos and Cephas. You do not belong to Martin Luther: Martin Luther belongs to you. You do not belong to John the Baptist, or John Calvin, or John Wesley, or John Paul II; they belong to you. The world, life, death, present, future—all belong to you. And you belong only to Christ. And Christ belongs to God.

This is the same ecumenical sermon, but this time not as warning or argument, but as a shout of triumph!

Gospel: Matt. 5:38–48. We continue the consideration of the righteousness which exceeds the righteousness of the scribes and Pharisees, which must be given us by God.

Vv. 38–42 may well be the most difficult in the Sermon on the Mount. Jesus cites the legal principle of proportional revenge. Then he suggests in its place something which goes beyond the no-revenge principle of the Holiness Code. It even goes beyond the principle of nonviolent resistance made famous by Gandhi. If we take Jesus literally, it is the principle of nonresistance. We are even to cooperate with the one who attacks us in our persons or our property. Most Christians cannot go along with that. It seems to them that the world cannot endure, that society must be a shambles, if we are not to defend ourselves personally and nationally. Here the wisdom of God really is folly.

But where have we arrived in following the wisdom of this world? At "assured mutual nuclear destruction." This is not a matter of defense at all. There is no defense against an all-out nuclear attack. Our present policy might be described as "revenge as deterrent." Each superpower assumes the other will not strike first because it knows the enemy can absorb that strike and retain the capability of vengeance, a return strike of equal savagery and destructiveness. Does this sound like wisdom, when we are contemplating human deaths in the hundreds of millions? Where is the real folly?

In calling us, Jesus offers us the liberating grace to rejoice when we are reviled and persecuted (Matt. 5:11–12). Does that liberate us from the necessity of defending ourselves? Maybe so. Does it liberate us from the necessity of defending others? Maybe not. This is a very difficult saying. But it surely calls into serious question the whole system of "defense" in which we are currently engaged as a nation. And it calls into question a "defensive" style of personal life whose chief concern is "don't let them take it away."

In vv. 43-48, Jesus moves beyond passive nonresistance to active love. He moves beyond the injunction of the Holiness Code to love our neighbors within the holy people of God. We are also to love our enemies. Because God loves his enemies, and the people of God should reflect the character of God. We may not imitate God in his omnipotence or his omnipresence. But we can imitate his grace. This is the perfection that is urged upon us in v. 48, a perfection of love that excludes no one.

Common Themes. The close connection between Leviticus 19 and Matthew 5 is unavoidable. We have already alluded to it many times: the move from no-vengeance to nonresistance; the move from love of neighbor to love of enemy. There is a clear parallel between "Be holy as I am holy" and "Be perfect as your Father is perfect." The basic shift lies in the recognition that God's love extends beyond his holy people to all people everywhere.

The Eighth Sunday after the Epiphany

Lutheran	Roman Catholic	Episcopal	Pres/UCC/Chr	Meth/COCU
Isa. 49:13–18	Isa. 49:14–15	Isa. 49:8–18	Isa. 49:14–18	Isa. 49:8–18
1 Cor. 4:1–13	1 Cor. 4:1–5	1 Cor. 4:1–5 (6–7) 8–13	1 Cor. 4:1–5	1 Cor. 4:1–13
Matt. 6:24–34	Matt. 6:24–34	Matt. 6:24–34	Matt. 6:24–34	Matt. 6:24–34

EXEGESIS

First Lesson: Isa. 49:8–18. Isa. 49:8–18 is quite similar to Isaiah 40: a way has been prepared in the desert (40:3) and the exiles return along that way (49:11); both chapters mention a shepherd (40:11, 49:9–10), mountains being leveled (40:3–4; 49:11), and consolation (40:1; 49:13). The reason for the similarity is that

Isaiah 49 begins the second half of Second Isaiah (49—55). There are also similarities between 42:1-13 and 49:7-18 (42:6b = 49:8b; 42:7 = 49:9a; 42:10-13 = 49:13). Well-known materials have been reworked and reapplied. The exiles in Babylon lament their fate; they express themselves in ways which are similar to Lamentations (49:7a, 14, 21, 24; cf. Lam. 1:1; 2:10-11; 3:16-18; 5:22; Isa. 40:27). Second Isaiah proclaims what the Lord is doing to change that fate and that therefore all creation should praise the Lord (49:13).

The form of this section is that of a proclamation of salvation: (1) a lament by the community is mentioned, (2) salvation is proclaimed, and (3) the result is affirmed (by someone). This pattern is found four times in this chapter: (1) 7a, (2) 8-12, and (3) 13 (7b probably also belongs with 13); (1) 14, (2) 15-19, and (3) 20; (1) 21, (2) 22-23a, and (3) 23b; (1) 24, (2) 25-26a, and (3) 26b. As is typical in a proclamation of salvation, Israel is the one to whom the Lord is speaking.

"In a time of favor" (49:8a; cf. 61:2), a common phrase in Jewish apocalyptic writing, means that time when the Lord takes pleasure in bringing salvation. A new exodus is described in 49:9a-11 (cf. Ps. 23). In modern Egypt, Syene (49:12) is Aswan; it marked the boundary between Egypt and Nubia in ancient times. Thus exiles will return not only from Babylon.

To draw an analogy between the Lord and a mother is not unique to Second Isaiah (49:15; cf. 66:13). The prophet uses the analogy to argue from the lesser to the greater: the steadfastness of a mother's love for her child is proverbial, but the Lord is even more steadfast (cf. 49:7b). The Lord cannot forget Zion, because he has tattooed its picture on the palms of his hands (49:16). The restoration is so sure that the prophet speaks of it as already taking place (49:17-18a). The Lord takes an oath (49:18b) that those who return will make Zion beautiful just as a bride is beautiful (cf. Jer. 2:32).

Second Lesson: 1 Cor. 4:1-13. Paul now applies what he has written in 1:10—3:23 to himself. Some in Corinth are clearly condemning him and his teaching (cf. 4:3, 5, 18; 3:21; 9:3). His response is that he and Apollos are not important in themselves, for they are simply servants and stewards, subordinates; they can only

The Eighth Sunday after the Epiphany

be judged by whether they do what their master commands, that is, by their faithfulness (4:1–2; cf. 3:10–11). Not even Paul's conscience is his final judge (4:3b–4; cf. Rom. 9:1; 2 Cor. 1:12), but the Lord alone, who at the last judgment will reward or withhold rewards (4:5; cf. 3:14–15; Rom. 2:29).

What Paul has written in 4:1–5 has been for the purpose of holding up to the Corinthian Christians the actual relationship between Apollos and himself as a model of Christian conduct (4:6a; cf. Phil. 4:9). "Puffed up" (4:6b; cf. 4:7b) describes the spiritual arrogance of some in Corinth (cf. 1:12, 29; 3:21; 4:18–19; 5:2) who hold that the eschaton has already arrived for them (4:8; cf. 2 Tim. 2:18). Paul responds with irony (4:8–10). The picture in 4:9 is that of wretched and despised persons sentenced to die in the arena. In 4:10 he repeats slogans from earlier in the letter (cf. 1:27–28; 3:18–19). The conclusion of the text is a typical Pauline list of tribulations (cf. Rom. 8:35; 2 Cor. 4:7–10; 6:4–5, 8–10; 11:16–33). The climax of the list is a pair of images describing that which is most miserable and least valuable (4:13b; these images might appropriately be translated "the world's garbage, the scum of the earth"). The whole final section of the text (4:9–13) is a summary of the theology of the cross; like Christ, his apostle is despised and persecuted, but he responds with love (cf. 13:4–7); his true strength is in the foolishness and weakness of the cross (cf. 4:10; 1:25; 2 Cor. 12:9–10).

Gospel: Matt. 6:24–34. Matt. 6:1–18 contrasts human and divine rewards; the general theme of 6:19–34 is single-minded devotion to the heavenly Father instead of material things. Matt. 6:24a is a proverbial saying; 6:24b applies it to the disciple's situation. The saying is based on the fact that according to the law at that time a slave could belong to two masters, which inevitably led to difficulties. In Jewish usage "mammon" did not mean something evil, but was a neutral word, like "property."

Matt. 6:25–31 is a doctrinal poem in parallel lines; it has two strophes, one about the birds and the other about the lilies. The refrain at the beginning and the end (6:25a and 31) creates a framework around the whole. Matt. 6:32–34 draws conclusions. The background for the poem is the wisdom tradition (cf. 5:45; Pss. 37:1–4, 25–26; 147:8–9); it is assumed that the reasoning will be self-evident to the listener. The argument has a typical rabbinic pattern: from the lesser to the greater (cf. 7:7-11). The text is not combating self-sufficiency as such, nor is it advocating passivity or, even less, resignation; it juxtaposes God and mammon, single-minded trust and anxiety (6:25, 27, 28, 31, 34). The one whose trust is in "property" of any kind is filled with anxiety, for he knows how insecure "property" is. The one who trusts in God is secure, for the unfailing Creator cares for him (cf. Phil. 4:6-7). Those with "little faith" (6:30) are not, to be sure, without any faith, but they obviously do not have a single-minded trust in the heavenly Father. "Cubit" (6:27) may be used to describe a short period of time.

Matt. 6:33 is a summary of Matthew's whole theology (and of the second through fourth petitions of the Lord's Prayer; cf. 6:10-11). The parallel between 6:32 and 6:33 indicates that an active "seeking" is meant. Furthermore, the text focuses on choosing between God and mammon, not on choosing between activity and passivity. As usual, Matthew is admonishing to action. God's ("his") kingdom will come in the future (cf. 5:20; 6:10; 7:21), as will God's ("his") righteousness (cf. 6:10b); the disciple is called upon single-mindedly ("first") to make them, not mammon, the goal of his actions (that is, do righteousness, cf. 5:20), and automatically "all" (cf. 6:32-33) other things will be cared for. Two witty proverbs (6:34) have been added at the close.

HOMILETICAL INTERPRETATION

First Lesson: Isa. 49:8-18. Our series of lessons from the prophets and the prophetic portions of the law ends as it began. It began on the Epiphany of Our Lord with a great shout of hope, the promise of Israel's restoration in Isaiah 60. Then we met the servant of the Lord and listened to the prophetic appeal for justice and loving loyalty. Now we are back again to the promise of restoration, this time in Isaiah 49. There are many powerful symbols of restoration in our lesson: the reapportionment of the land (v. 8); the release of prisoners who sit in darkness (v. 9; cf. Isa. 42:7; 58:6); the leading and feeding of the people as a flock (vv. 9 and 10; cf. Isa. 40:11); the making of a highway in the wilderness (v. 11; cf. Isa. 40:3-4); the gathering again of the exiles (vv. 12 and 18); the builders outstripping the destroyers (v. 17).

The Eighth Sunday after the Epiphany

The promise of restoration comes to those who live with an acute sense of the absence of God: "The Lord has forsaken me, my Lord has forgotten me" (v. 14 RSV). See the exegesis for an understanding of how this lament is repeated throughout the chapter and how it echoes the Book of Lamentations.

God is not absent, says the prophet. He is on the way with the promised restoration. The basis for this confidence is not this or that development in history but who God is! And in pressing this point, the prophet uses feminine imagery for God. If a woman cannot forget her sucking child, how much more impossible is it for God to forget you. Like a tattoo on the palms of the hands, so Jerusalem is imprinted on the memory and concern of God. He cannot and will not wash his hands of you.

All the furor a few years back about the death of God was a sign that we too live in a time of the absence of God. Pick up the front page of any newspaper and the question is unavoidable: where is God? (Cf. Ps. 42:3.) We should not duck the question on the grounds that it is not properly pious to ask it. Jesus asked it: "My God, my God, why have you forsaken me?" The answer must lie for us, as for Israel, in the character of God. A macho, James Bond–type God might well say: "Sure, I've forsaken you. What do you expect after what you've done to me?" But a God who is feminine as well as masculine and who knows what a mother feels toward her sucking child cannot and will not abandon us. That God will restore us.

What would constitute restoration for us in our day? Here the preacher needs a consecrated imagination. The restoration of a ruined environment? Of our decayed inner cities? Of confidence in our government, our institutions, and ourselves? Of lost innocence and idealism? Of old virtues and moral standards? Of a simpler and sturdier way of life? Of compassion for "the tired, the poor, the huddled masses yearning to breathe free"?

Second Lesson: 1 Cor. 4:1–13. From the high point at the end of chap. 3, Paul descends to a passage in which he defends himself and chides his critics. But there are precious insights here, too.

"Stewards of the mysteries of God." What a sermon topic! You've preached doubtless on the stewardship of time, talent, and money. Perhaps you've dealt with the stewardship of energy and earth. But stewards of the mysteries of God? The mysteries are God's secrets

(Eph. 3:1–13) which have been opened to us (Mark 4:11). We are not to keep those secrets hidden within the walls of the church, couched in "churchy" language, concealed in obscure rites and ceremonies. Not to share God's secrets is just as poor stewardship as if we ate all the bread and drank all the wine that belonged to our fellow servants (cf. Luke 12:42–46) or hoarded all our money (cf. Luke 16:10–11). No more than bread or money do the mysteries of God belong to us. The church holds them in trust for the world. We fulfill our stewardship by proclaiming them plainly and powerfully (cf. 1 Cor. 2:4). They do not bestow on us a vaunted superiority over the world, only a solemn responsibility to be found trustworthy.

"What have you that you did not receive?" (v. 7 RSV). Here is the basic text for stewardship of all kinds. Until people see and acknowledge this simple truth, extracting money or time or service or anything from them is like extracting an impacted wisdom tooth! Note that the opposite of stewardship is boasting. In today's consumer culture, how often we seek to establish status on the basis of what we own. To admit we own nothing strikes very radically at the roots of our pride.

The passage ends with an eloquent comparison between the satiated, affluent, regal life-style to which the Corinthians aspire and the life-style of true apostles who become "the refuse of the world, the offscouring of all things" (v. 13 RSV). It is most instructive to compare the description of the apostles here with the description of the truly blessed in the Beatitudes (Matt. 5:3–12).

Gospel: Matt. 6:24–34. We began our series on the Sermon on the Mount with the assertion that the sermon is a proclamation of the grace of God rather than a promulgation of a new and more stringent law. In today's lesson, God's grace is reaffirmed in matchless, unforgettable mini-parables. The birds of the air do not sow or reap or gather into barns, yet your heavenly Father feeds them. That's grace! The lilies of the field do not toil or spin, yet Solomon in all his glory was not arrayed like one of these. That's grace! Jesus argues from these illustrations, as the exegesis points out, with characteristic rabbinic logic: if this, how much more that. If God is this gracious to birds and flowers, how much more gracious will he be to you.

God's grace carries with it a demand: we should choose to serve

God and refuse to serve mammon (v. 24). To serve mammon is to make what we shall eat or drink or wear the central concern of life (vv. 25, 31). To serve God is to seek first his kingdom and his righteousness (v. 33). The question is not one of prudence and planning but, as Tillich so well put it, of "ultimate concern."

God's grace also carries with it a promise: freedom from anxiety (vv. 25, 27, 28, 31, 34). Ask any counselor or psychiatrist about the toll that anxiety takes. Our lesson ends with a very practical hint. We can lay hold on the promised freedom from anxiety if we will live in day-tight compartments (v. 34). Alcoholics Anonymous discovered this long ago. It is impossible for an alcoholic to stay sober all the rest of her or his life. But the most strongly addicted can stay sober today. Just today.

Common Themes. God's care for the birds and the flowers (Matt. 6) is really an answer to the absence of God (Isa. 49). To serve mammon is to live as though God were dead. Stewardship, admitting we have nothing we did not receive (1 Cor. 4), is living like the birds and flowers. Boasting in what we have, refusing to live as stewards, is living like the Gentiles and serving mammon.

The Transfiguration of Our Lord
The Last Sunday after the Epiphany

Lutheran	Roman Catholic	Episcopal	Pres/UCC/Chr	Meth/COCU
Exod. 24:12, 15–18	Dan. 7:9–10, 13–14	Exod. 24:12 (13–14), 15–18	Ezek. 34:11–17	Exod. 24:12–18
2 Pet. 1:16–19 (20–21)	2 Pet. 1:16–19	Phil. 3:7–14	1 Cor. 15:20–28	2 Pet. 1:16–21
Matt. 17:1–9	Matt. 17:1–9	Matt. 17:1–9	Matt. 25:31–46	Matt. 17:1–9

EXEGESIS

First Lesson: Exod. 24:12–18. Exod. 24:15b continues the Priestly account broken off in 19:2, and 24:15b–18a introduces the Priestly account of the ritual prescriptions for the tabernacle in

Exodus 25—31. Exod. 24:14 points forward to 31:18—32:6, the account of the acts of the people while Moses was on the mountain. There is a general consensus that 24:15b–18a comes from the Priestly source, which was compiled between the captivity in 587 B.C. and some time in the fifth century B.C.

In Exodus 24 "coming up" and "going up" are often mentioned; gradually the "people" and the "elders" are left behind and Moses alone ascends to the top, although in the end the people also see the fire at the top of the mountain (24:17). The words "with the law and the commandment" (24:12b) have been added later, since only the Ten Commandments were written by the Lord and given to Moses (cf. 31:18; 32:15–16; 34:1). In 24:13b Moses goes up the mountain before speaking to the elders (24:14); then in 24:15b Moses goes up the mountain again.

Joshua, as the future leader of the people, goes up part of the mountain with Moses (cf. 32:17). Aaron and Hur had held up Moses' hands during the battle with the Amalekites (cf. 17:10, 12). Forty is a number used to indicate a relatively long period of time; according to Deut. 9:9 Moses spent the time fasting.

The word "settle" (24:16) is "tent" in Hebrew; the transcendent Lord does not "dwell" on earth, for that would be too human, too immanent, but he does "tent" among us. (The Greek word for "dwell" in John 1:14 is "tent.") The Priestly editor is concerned throughout to avoid idolatry and yet to describe how and where the Lord is truly present. The Lord meets Moses and the people at Sinai and in the tabernacle (tent of meeting); he comes as his glory, which means his power, majesty, honor, revelation, light, and even himself, his presence (cf. 33:22; Lev. 9:4, 6, 23). His glory, which looks like fire and light, is always surrounded by a cloud. The cloud covers Sinai or the tabernacle, and the glory remains inside (cf. Exod. 40:34–35, 38). The origin of the concept of glory described here may be the experience of an active volcano (cf. Exod. 19:16–18; a different picture lies behind 24:9–11). The response by the people to the glory of the Lord is fear in both senses of the term: terror and respect.

Second Lesson: 2 Pet. 1:16–21. Second Peter is written in the form of a last will and testament (cf. Testaments of the Twelve Patriarchs; John 14—17; Acts 20:18-35; 2 Timothy). It is also pseudonymous; at the time when Second Peter was written, writing under a pseudonym was not understood to be dishonest. Rather, the apostolic faith was being handed on, and the fact that the author uses Peter's name is an indication of the authority people at that place and time attributed to Peter. Paul's letters have at least a quasi-canonical status (3:15-16), which is one of several indications that Second Peter was written in the first half of the second century.

The author writes against those who deny the second coming of Christ (3:3-4) and who reject salvation history and put "cleverly devised myths" (1:16a; cf. 1 Tim. 1:4; 4:7; 2 Tim. 4:4; Titus 1:14) in its place. Over against these opponents, he claims proof for the validity of his own position because he (assuming the role of Peter) and the other apostles both saw and heard (1:16a, 18a) what happened at the transfiguration and because their experience is a fulfillment of OT prophecy (1:19a).

Only apostles were present at the transfiguration, and consequently this event enhances apostolic authority. The transfiguration account emphasizes that the apostles heard the confirmation of Christ's divine sonship with the Father ("majesty," 1:16b; "honor and glory," 1:17a; cf. 1:3a); this is a prefigurement of the fact that there will be a second coming and of what each believer can expect to be his reward at the final end (cf. 1:4b).

No specific prophecy in the OT is referred to (1:19a); the whole OT is understood as prophecy (cf. 1 Pet. 1:10). At this point the author shifts from the first person plural (= the apostles, 1:1b) to the second person plural (= his readers, 19b-21) and warns about the correct interpretation of prophecy (cf. 3:15-16). Prophecy is inspired by the Holy Spirit, and therefore only those who have the Holy Spirit are able to interpret it (1:20-21); the implication is that the opponents do not and that only the official church has the correct interpretation, which is the apostolic tradition (cf. 1:1b).

Gospel: Matt. 17:1-9. Matthew's concern is christological; God himself confirms the revelation which has just been made to Peter and confessed by him (16:16-17). The story is not a resurrection narrative which has been displaced, for it lacks the form of such a narrative, and in no resurrection narrative is Jesus accompanied by other witnesses. Nor is this a miracle story, for here something is done to Jesus instead of by him. Instead, this is haggadic midrash (reflection about history by means of OT passages) which has the purpose of explicating who Jesus is.

The immediate background is the Feast of Tabernacles (cf. Lev. 23:39–43), as is evident from the "booths" (17:4) and the "six days" (17:1); the six days refer both to the six days between the Day of Atonement and the Feast of Tabernacles and to the six days leading up to the climactic seventh day of the Feast of the Tabernacles, a day filled with messianic hopes (cf. Lev. 23:27, 34; John 7:2, 37). But other associations are intended. The most obvious is the giving of the law at Mount Sinai, which has a mountain, six days, a cloud (Exod. 24:15–18), and a transformation (Exod. 34:29, 35); thus Jesus is the new Moses. For Elijah Mount Sinai had also been a place of revelation (1 Kings 19:8–18), and a mountain is a traditional place of revelation (cf. 5:1; 15:29; 28:16). For Matthew the Law and the Prophets, Moses and Elijah, are witnesses to Jesus (17:3; cf. Mark 9:4, where Mark has the order Elijah and Moses; Rev. 11:3–6). It was expected that at the end "the glory of the Lord and the cloud will appear" (2 Macc. 2:8; cf. 2 Esd. 7:97; Syr. Apoc. Bar. 51:3, 5, 10; Rev. 1:16; 14:14). The voice from the cloud (17:5; cf. 3:17) echoes Isa. 42:1; Ps. 2:7; and Deut. 18:15.

Matthew, as is typical for him, presents the disciples in a better light than Mark; Peter does know what to say (17:4; cf. Mark 9:6). At a theophany fear is the normal reaction (17:6; cf. 14:26; 28:4; Dan. 8:17; 10:10; Rev. 1:17), and the fear is removed by a touch and words of comfort (17:7; cf. Isa. 6:7; Dan. 10:16–19; Rev. 1:17). The exhortation "listen to him" (17:5b) for Matthew would refer to "all that I have commanded you" (28:20a), that is, Jesus' ethical teaching; like Moses (Deut. 18:15), Jesus is both prophet and legislator.

HOMILETICAL INTERPRETATION

Here for the first time since the Baptism of Our Lord, one lesson is clearly central. Matt. 17:1–9 records the transfiguration, and that is what we celebrate today.

The transfiguration is, of course, *the* epiphany, *the* revealing of the hidden glory of Jesus. Here more surely and fully than in the adoration of the wise men or the descent of the dove at baptism, the surface appearance of things swings open and the ultimate depth of reality is revealed. A face shining like the sun and garments white as light are marks of a heavenly being. The transcendent, all-powerful Son of man of Rev. 1:12–16 now shines through the humble, earthly Jesus who is on his way to the cross. The true meaning of his altogether human life is revealed in the bright cloud that overshadows him and the voice that speaks of him as the beloved Son in whom God is well pleased—the very words that occur also at the epiphany-baptism (see the interpretation under the Baptism of Our Lord, the First Sunday after the Epiphany, above).

We are in the realm of vision here. Matt. 17:9 uses the word *horama*, "vision." High mountains, clouds, and a voice from heaven are characteristics of biblical vision-stories. We find them all in Exod. 24:12–18. The reaction of the witnesses is the classic human reaction to what Rudolf Otto has called "the numinous"—that seldom-seen hidden depth of reality that makes us tremble, yet fascinates us. They fall on their faces, filled with awe (cf. Rev. 1:17).

How do we preach on a vision, on an experience of the numinous, on an undiluted epiphany? The experience of the three apostles may well be quite foreign to most of the congregation and even to the preacher. One is tempted to ignore what is central and difficult and to preach around the edges: we all have mountaintop experiences, but we must not try to prolong them, because there are demons to be cast out in the valley below. That may be true, but it misses the center.

Certainly one thing at stake in the transfiguration experience is the authority of Jesus. Moses (the Law) and Elijah (the Prophets) are figures of overwhelming authority for the apostles, and for us, if we take the OT seriously. But Jesus emerges as a figure of greater authority. "My beloved Son . . . listen to him," says the heavenly voice (v. 5). And when Moses and Elijah have disappeared, Jesus remains (v. 8). The authority of Jesus is precisely the lesson that the writer of 2 Peter draws from the transfiguration experience. Our faith is not a "cleverly devised myth" (2 Pet. 1:16); it is rather "the prophetic word made more sure" (2 Pet. 1:19). Jesus has authority because he has received honor and glory from God the Father (2 Pet. 1:17).

If Jesus' authority is greater than the authority of the Law and the Prophets, then we cannot accept a biblicism that puts all Scripture on a single level. The authority of Jesus, revealed on the mount of transfiguration, provides us with an internal principle of biblical interpretation. He does not come to abolish the Law and the Prophets, but to fulfill them (Matt. 5:17). In every perplexing question, his authority is final: "It was said . . . but I say unto you."

Though a transfiguration is not a common experience, the problem of conflicting authorities and the hunger for true authority are common experiences for us all. Here is a handle the preacher can seize.

Another way of preaching on the transfiguration is to see it as the proper preface to Lent. There is a profound insight in its position in the lectionary. Jesus can go his way to the cross because his understanding of himself as suffering servant, so vehemently contradicted by Peter (Matt. 16:22), is confirmed by the Law and the Prophets and above all by the voice from heaven. To take or to avoid a course that will lead to a cross is a decision all of us face. And that common experience gives us another handle for preaching on the transfiguration.

A third way of preaching on the transfiguration is to see it as an experience of worship. That is clearly one level of meaning in Exodus 24; even more clearly in Revelation 4—5. All such epiphanies, including Matt. 17:1-8, are models for the worship of Israel and of the church. Worship is something distinct from the more ordinary experiences of life (on a high mountain apart). In worship we see the hidden reality behind the appearance of things (transfigured before them). In worship the ordinary boundaries of time are transcended (Moses and Elijah are present). In worship we get clear about where the real authority is, we are filled with awe, and we are healed. In every other reference to the touch of Jesus in Matthew, it is a healing touch. So it is also here in v. 7. We rise from worship to resume the way to the cross in a world full of suffering. But we have seen who Jesus really is and he has shown us that we do not need to be afraid.